PAGES FROM A WELSH CUNNING MAN'S BOOK

Also by Andrew Phillip Smith

Gnostic Tendencies (Bardic Press)
John the Baptist and the Last Gnostics (Watkins Publishing)
Lost Teachings of the Cathars (Watkins Publishing)
Secret History of the Gnostics (Watkins Publishing)
A Dictionary of Gnosticism (Quest)
Gnostic Writings on the Soul: Annotated & Explained
The Lost Sayings of Jesus: Annotated & Explained
The Gospel of Philip: Annotated & Explained (all Skylight Paths)

Also Available from Bardic Press

Other Voices of Gnosticism
Voices of Gnosticism
Miguel Conner
*The Gnostic: A Journal of Gnosticism, Western Esotericism
and Spirituality 1–6*
Spirit Possession and the Origins of Christianity
Stevan Davies
Revolt of the Widows
Stevan Davies
The Gospel of Thomas and Christian Wisdom
Stevan Davies
Hedges, Ditches and Dreams
Alastair Ashford-Brown
Visit our website at www.bardicpress.com
email us at bardicpress@gmail.com

PAGES FROM A WELSH CUNNING MAN'S BOOK

Magic and Fairies in Nineteenth-Century Wales

Andrew Phillip Smith

Bardic Press

About the Author

Andrew Phillip Smith was born in 1966, comes from Penarth, and attended the University College of Swansea. He is the author of *Pages From a Welsh Cunning Man's Book: Magic and Fairies in Nineteenth-Century Wales* and several books on Gnosticism, including *Lost Teachings of the Cathars*, *Secret History of the Gnostics*, and *A Dictionary of Gnosticism*. He is publisher of Bardic Press and was editor of *The Gnostic: A Journal of Gnosticism, Western Esotericism and Spirituality*. He now lives in a late eighteenth-century Glamorgan cottage, two minutes walk from the grave of a family of wizards, which was an undertaker's residence for 50 years and may well have a ghost.

Acknowledgments

Robat Gruffydd for permission to quote from *Byd y Dyn Hysbys* by Kate Bosse-Griffiths. Oli Foster for permission to include the phtograph of the cattle protection charm and his grandfather's article on the charm.

David Rankine, David Conway, Ronald Hutton, Mhara Starling Kristoffer Hughes and Joseph Peterson variously for endorsements, encouragement and discussion of the text and the book.

Tessa Finn for proofreading and everything else. The Welsh Occult Conference and the Dragons for hosting my talks on Welsh magic. The staff of the National Library of Wales.

And to all the dynion a menywod hysbys, gorffennol, presennol a dydodol.

Copyright © 2023 Andrew Phillip Smith
Printed on acid-free paper
Published by Bardic Press
(Check website for mailing address)
http://www.bardicpress.com
andrew@bardicpress.com
ISBN 978-1-906834-46-3

Bardic Press
Wesley House
Church Road
Cadoxton
Barry
CF63 1JY
Wales

Contents

Introduction	1
Llyfr Cyfrin y Dyn Hysbys o Sir Ddinbych	15
Tylwyth Teg and Dynion Hysbys	73
Wizards, Witches and Fairies	90
The Seven Sisters Spell	122
Magic in Denbighshire	135
Siôn y Rhose	154
Siôn Gyfarwydd	160
Bewitched Cattle	170
Geomancy in Llyfr Cyfrin	198
Appendices	
Dewinesau Dinbych	206
The Witches of Denbigh	206
Welsh Astrologers, Sorcerers, &C-	214
Further Reading	219
Index	224

Introduction

Llyfr Cyfrin: a 'secret book'. What could be more interesting than a secret book full of magical spells? How about a secret book that has disappeared?

Llyfr Cyfrin y Dyn Hysbys o Sir Ddinbych, 'The Secret Book of the Cunning Man of Denbighshire,' was the title given by Kate Bosse-Griffiths to a small manuscript notebook from the nineteenth century. The book contained strange symbols and invocations, spells and other magical material in both Welsh and English. Thin leather was stretched across the cover and it had traces of coal dust. The notebook shows an especial interest in the magical summoning of the Tylwyth Teg, the fair folk, who are the Welsh fairies. This includes a spell to summon seven fairy sisters who were known to magicians for centuries before this manuscript. This Welsh interest in fairy magic itself persisted for centuries beyond the equivalent interest in fairy magic in England.

The association of the notebook with nineteenth-century Denbighshire connects it with the larger-than-life historical characters who were known as witches, soothsayers, cattle healers, fortunetellers and fraudsters. Denbighshire was also the location of the most famous magical site in nineteenth century Wales, Ffynnon Elian, the well of St Elian, notorious for being used not for healing, as were the many other wells dedicated to Welsh saints, but for cursing. One man mentioned in the notebook has a direct link to Ffynnon Elian.

Only one book has so far reproduced extracts from the Llyfr Cyfrin, Kate Bosse-Griffiths' *Byd y Dyn Hysbys* ('The World of the Cunning Man'), which was published in 1977, and, to my knowledge, no one has seen it since.[1]

Her book reintroduced Welsh readers to the concept of the dyn hysbys, the most common name for the magical practitioners in Wales who performed a variety of tasks for their communities and have an equivalent in England and elsewhere in the cunning man or cunning folk.[2] The repertoire of their activities included divination, finding lost objects, the healing of both people and animals and the undoing of curses or breaking of malign witchcraft. Many charged fees for their work, others only accepted gifts in exchange for successful operations. Closely linked to cunning folk were the swynwr or swynwraig[3], charmers who might only have a small number of traditional charms. Consurwyr (conjurors) also performed many of these tasks but were noted or notorious for consorting with spirits.

In nine brief chapters Kate Bosse-Grittiths outlines the concept of the dyn hysbys, offers some of the biography and folklore surround the Harrieses of Cwrt-y-cadno in Carmarthenshire, the most famous dynion hysbys of the nineteenth century, relates some tales of similar figures, describes the physical notebook and contents of *Llyfr Cyfrin y Dyn Hysbys o Sir Ddinbych*, includes some other charms and symbols and makes some broad comparisons with somewhat similar traditions worldwide. Long out of print, hard to find and only ever published in Welsh, *Byd y Dyn Hysbys* has long had a certain aura of mystery to it.

Kate Bosse-Griffiths discovered the Secret Book

through her friend Llinos Davies. The dedication of *Byd y Dyn Hysbys* reads, 'Cyflwynedig i Llinos, a ddangosodd y ffordd i mi', 'Dedicated to Llinos, who showed me the way.' In her list of sources at the end of the book, Bosse-Griffiths includes the manuscript of Llyfr Cyfrin under the category 'Llawysgrifau yn y Llyfrgell Genedlaethol Aberystwyth,' 'manuscripts in the National Library Aberystwyth,' but notes in parentheses that it is 'ym meddiant Llinos Davies', 'in the possession of Llinos Davies.' Llinos Davies, a good friend of Kate Bosse-Griffiths and her family, was curator of rare books at University College of Wales, Swansea, my own alma mater. It seems that the manuscript book remained in her possession but its whereabouts are unknown. She passed away in 1998. Neither Swansea University rare books department nor the archives department knew of the book when I enquired. Other researchers have checked the National Library at Aberystwyth to no avail. It may seem odd that such a notable volume might have disappeared, yet at the end of *Byd y Dyn Hysbys* Kate Bosse-Griffiths describes a conversation with Cecil Price, lecturer in English at UCW Swansea.

> And then, to my great surprise, the Professor confessed, 'I bought a small book like that about ten years ago in Ralph's secondhand bookshop in Swansea – a book written by hand towards the beginning of the previous century. It's full of instructions concerning methods for placing and removing enchantments and astrological signs. I'm sure that the old wizards copied notes from each other.'

My heartbeat grew faster: another book from the time of John Harries, Cwrt-y-cadno, possibly from south Wales, came to light in a shop in Swansea? I asked about getting to see it soon, before this booklet went to press.

The professor agreed kindly, but there was a difficulty. He was not sure he could put his hands on the booklet at once. Ten years was a long time for someone who usually bought books almost every day, and the professor had forgotten where he had placed the little booklet. But he would look for it. And so it was necessary to wait. But I am sure that more books like this are available from the same period. Further, in the near future, someone will have the chance to compare them, discovering new knowledge on the hidden life that flourished in the beginning of the last century, contemporary with the beginning of the National eisteddfod, and the Industrial Revolution. and the Nonconformist Religious Revival.[4]

As far as we know she never did get to read Cecil Price's little booklet. So not one but two Welsh magical manuscripts were in private hands in Swansea in the 1970s and both of them are, as far as we know, lost.

Kate Bosse-Griffiths

Kate Bosse-Griffiths was an extraordinary woman, a German of Jewish ancestry who came to Wales as a refugee. She married a Welshman, learned Welsh and raised a Welsh-speaking family who would themselves go on to become very influential in Welsh language and literature. She established a Welsh literary circle, wrote several novels in Welsh and many non-fiction articles on archaeology and folklore in Welsh and English. She helped to establish the Egyptian Centre which is now at Swansea University. She was born Käthe Bosse in Wittenberg in 1910 to Paul Bosse (1881-1947) and Käthe Bosse (née Ledien, 1886-1944). Her father Paul was a doctor whose background was ethnically German. Her mother Käthe, though raised Lutheran in a family that was already Christianised, was descended from Jews on both side of her family.[5]

Paul Bosse, like many others, juggled the survival of his family with his ethical concerns about the behaviour of the Nazis. He was one of the doctors who gave medical assistance to the German sprinters in the 1936 Munich Olympics which were notoriously intended as a propaganda exercise for Nazi Germany.

Kate trained as an Egyptologist and secured a position at the Berlin State Museum in Berlin. She lost the job in 1936 because of her Jewish ancestry. In the same year Kate's mother Käthe found herself unable to work in her husband's clinic due to the increasing restrictions on the involvement of Jews in daily life.

Kate left for Britain with the aid of a French organisation that helped German Jews. After a brief period in St Andrews in Scotland she lived in Oxford where she was offered a position and then a fellowship at the Ashmolean Museum. There she fell in love with a Welshman, J. Gwyn Griffiths, and moved to Wales, living initially in Bettws-y-Coed in north Wales. She married Gwyn in September 1939 and raised a family, living first in Pentre in the Rhondda, but settling long term in Swansea. In the Rhondda they established a Welsh-language literary circle, Cylch Cadwgan, which in addition to Kate and Gwyn, who were both writers, included Rhydwen Williams, Pennar Davies and others. She progressed quickly in learning Welsh. By 1941 she had already had a novel published in Welsh. Kate became a prolific writer in both Welsh and English, publishing several novels and volumes of short stories in Welsh and many short articles in English on a wide variety of historical and archaeological subjects, but her field of expertise remained Egyptology and in 1947 she was appointed Honorary Curator of the Archaeological Department of the Royal Institution, Swansea. In 1965-66 she spent a year at Cairo University. She published what may be the only book in Welsh on Egyptology, *Tywysennau o'r Aifft* ('Ears of Corn from Egypt', Llyfrau'r Dryw, 1970.)

In 1971 she was appointed Honorary Curator of the Wellcome Museum at University College, Swansea, holding the post until 1995. She established a collection of Egyptian antiquities donated by the Wellcome Trust which eventually became the Egyptian Centre, a lovely small museum in the Singleton Campus which is popular with schools and other visitors.

Gwyn was a Christian pacifist in the Welsh nonconformist tradition of pacifism. He registered as a conscientious objector during the Second World War and worked on the land. Kate's mother Käthe was imprisoned and died in Ravensbruck concentration camp in 1944. Other family members died in the persecutions.

In 1943 Robat was born, and in 1946 Heini. Both of her sons contributed to Welsh-language culture, Heini as a teacher or tutor of Welsh, who is well-known for his books on learning Welsh such as *Welcome to Welsh* and *Welsh Rules*. Robat co-founded Y Lolfa ('The Lounge'), a publishing house that has published a wide range of books, from memoirs and histories to recipe books and *Lol*, the annual satirical magazine published at the time of the National Eisteddfod. Y Lolfa is still a major publisher of Welsh-language and Welsh-interest material.

Kate died in 1998 in Morriston Hospital aged 87. Her most visible legacy is the Egyptian Museum at Swansea. She came back into the public eye in Wales again in 2013 with the publication of *Yr Erlid* ('The Persecution'), a book by her son Heini, published by Y Lolfa, that documents the fortunes of her family as Jews or people of Jewish descent in 20th century Germany. It won the Welsh Book of the Year prize for 2013 and was published in English as *A Haven From Hitler* in 2014. While she wrote a wide range of material in Welsh and English, *Byd y Dyn Hysbys* (Y Lolfa, 1977) stands out as unusual as an at that time unique investigation into the popular tradition of Welsh magic.[6]

Byd y Dyn Hysbys was a general exploration of Welsh cunning folk, not an edition of the Llyfr Cyfrin, and Bosse-Griffiths only excerpted short sections from it. There may be several factors involved in this: she may have had difficulty transcribing some of the text; much of the material may not have all that been interesting to her or her intended audience; and, crucially, her book was in Welsh and she was not inclined to include too much of the English-language material that took up around four fifths of the notebook.

The Llyfr Cyfrin contains a variety of material typical of the interests of the nineteenth century dyn hysbys. Of particular note are the rituals that summon the Tylwyth Teg, the Welsh fairies, other spells that involved evocation of spirits and a brief journal entry that describes the cure of bewitched cattle for a farmer. Cunning folk were noted for the books that they owned, sometimes amounting to extensive libraries, which not only impressed their clients, who might more often than not be illiterate, but also provided them with knowledge and techniques beyond the simple charms that were their stock in trade.

I have been able to trace the origin of, or at least antecedents for just about everything included in the notebook. Kate Bosse-Griffiths only included material that she wished to discuss, and thus the extracts from the Llyfr Cyfrin are inserted piecemeal into various sections of *Byd y Dyn Hysbys*. She also included photographic reproductions of five pages. I noticed that half of one of the reproduced pages had not been included in the main text and so I was able to transcribe and insert that material. My discovery of her sources has also allowed me to reconstruct other sections of the Llyfr Cyfrin.

Why did Kate write *Byd y Dyn Hysbys*? Why was an Egyptologist interested in the practitioners of Welsh folk magic?[7] Kate herself wrote an odd passage in *Byd y Dyn Hysbys*

> And after having learned 'the trade of winds' for seven years as a disciple of the cunning men of Wales, I see that the time has come to reveal my final and amazing experience, that invisible means can have visible effects, that

Divinity is the beginning of everything and that there is meaning in everything.[8]

While this seems at least partly tongue-in-cheek, it does suggest that she appreciated what she saw as the non-Christian point of view of the dynion hysbys. She was also interested in the Greek Magical Papyrii, practical magical material written in Greek (and also in the Coptic and Demotic forms of the Egyptian language) during the period of the Roman occupation of Egypt. Kate was not the only one in her family who was fascinated by magic. Gwyn wrote two articles about a case of folk magic in the Rhondda in 1937.[9] These articles described a magical ritual performed by two spinster sisters in order to prevent their brother from marrying and leaving the family home. The two sisters disliked their brother's fiancée and were worried about the loss of a man about the house.

> In an industrial village in south Wales, about four years ago, two sisters were living with their brother. They heard that their brother was probably marrying and leaving them; and his chosen girl was undesirable for other reasons. They were looking for a way to stop him in his marital intentions. Finally one of them went to a witch dewines who used to tell people's fortunes and also gave instructions for charming. She said there was a way to stop the marriage. The women at midnight (at twelve exactly) had to take half a bucket of fine coal, lay on it ten large spoons of salt, and add to the heap some of their own water; then toss it all over the kitchen fire, and wait to watch it dry. Doing this regularly for a couple of months, it was said, would result in the brother separating from his girlfriend. They did so diligently for the allotted time, though the sisters had some trouble hiding it from their brother. (Once he got out of bed just before midnight and was surprised to see them preparing to feed the fire at that time.) Nevertheless, she married the brother, and indeed did so sooner than expected. I

can assure the truth of this story. (I got it from a friend who knew the shopkeeper who sold the much needed salt until the sisters felt they should explain the endless purchases.)[10]

Gwyn points out how salt was used in a Welsh folktale in which a gŵr cyfarwydd, a cunning man, restores a changeling who was taken by the Tylwyth Teg and goes on to compare the magical techniques with a spell in the Greek Magical Papyrri in which urine was used.[11]

This book began as an appendix to another book that is still in preparation about a much longer printed collection of Welsh magic also from the 1830s. I then decided to work on the current book as an interim project, thinking of it as little more than a pamphlet that I could dash off and then get back to my main task. Instead, I discovered that there was a wealth of tradition available on all aspects of the Llyfr Cyfrin, from fairy magic and Denbighshire wizards and witches to cattle bewitching. I found myself obsessively tracking down the sources used by the dyn hysbys.

I have supplied plenty of supporting material that fleshes out the world of the early nineteenth century dyn hysbys. Welsh magicians liaised with the Tylwyth Teg long after their English counterparts had lost interest in their own fairies. Folklore and court records offer differing proportions of fantasy and reality in their accounts of the dyn hysbys' relations with the Tylwyth Teg.

Kate Bosse-Griffiths believed the dyn hysbys of the notebook to be from Denbighshire because he met, according to his own account, with a farmer named Allwood in Wrexham. Thus I have included some of the rich magical folklore traditions surrounding Denbighshire along with memories and folktales of the eccentric characters who were the witches and wizards of that county.

The Llyfr Cyfrin tells us that the dyn hysbys cured

the farmer's bewitched cattle, but does not tell us what method he used, therefore I offer some extensive material on the methods used to unwitch cattle and suggest that the Llyfr Cyfrin itself may contain the symbol used to prevent witchcraft. The author mentions in passing a competitor of his, a dyn hysbys of the name Shon y Rhoses, who turns out to have been a notorious fraudster commemorated in court records and associated with the cursing well of Ffynnon Elian.

We do not know who is the author of the Llyfr Cyfrin, but I make a stab at an identification. Even if I am wrong, the suggested author is very similar in his interests and methods to the dyn hysbys who compiled the Llyfr Cyfrin.

I include the surviving text of the Llyfr Cyfrin with an English translation and suggest a reconstruction of some of the contents mentioned in passing by Kate Bosse-Griffiths. Extensive notes offer comparative material and context to the contents of the Llyfr Cyfrin.

On the whole I take the reported experiences and understandings of the supernatural at face value, unless there is obvious fraud involved, as is the case in some of the court records. The reader may wonder what my attitudes are to matters such as the reality of magic and fairies. Yes, I do believe that magic can be effectatious. And I do believe that people can have genuine experiences for which the contemporary cultural explanation is an encounter with the fairies. No, I don't believe that someone could have been physically transported fifty miles through his contact with the fairies. Nor do I believe that illnesses of cattle or a failure to churn butter are the result of witchcraft, even though I may seem to state these in a matter of fact way. If people believed that a cow was bewitched I merely go along with it as part of a loosely phenomenological description of people's concerns. The kinds of folk tales which are told more generally as stories to entertain are exceptions to this rule.

By the end of the project I was feeling pretty smug with myself for having tracked down sources for nearly everything in the notebook, yet also a little disenchanted: some of the material is taken from contemporary printed sources, while even the fairy magic is adapted from early modern rituals that were in Latin or English. Yet that is what we should expect. Wales has never been just an obscure linguistic outpost on the farther side of an island cut off from the European mainland. From the time of the Roman invasion, and even earlier, it has always been in relationship with the rest of Britain and Ireland and been a part of a general western European culture. England had cunning folk too, Europe had service magicians, yet the dynion hysbys had a particular range of interests and traditions and a particularly Welsh relationship to magic and community. Each time I dug a little deeper I found that the material related to Welsh experiences and traditions. Whether you are interested in a Welsh perspective or in fairy lore or in magical practices, I hope this book will offer a glimpse into a world full of magical belief and practice that was gradually eroded by the practical yet disenchanted benefits of industrialism and rationality.

Notes

1 Richard Suggett commented,
'Conjurors compiled their own manuscript books of recipes, charms and incantations, and a few have survived... The most interesting of these manuscripts is the secret book ("llyfr Cyfrin") of an unnamed Denbighshire wise-man. This stubby volume has been described by Kate Bosse Griffiths: it has 200 pages but was small enough to fit in the pocket of a great coat. The contents were written in Welsh and English and included several conjuring formulae to summon the spirits called fairies (tylwyth teg); a formula to invocate and converse with spirits of the dead; methods of telling fortunes through astrology; and various charms in English and Welsh, one with the note that these "words being spoke with grate revarens and faith has don wonders"...'
Richard Suggett, *A History of Magic and Witchcraft in Wales* (The History Press, 2008) p.99-100.
2 The Welsh terms for these practitioners were chiefly dyn hysbys or menyw hysbys, gŵr cyfarwydd or menyw gyfarwydd. The English equivalents are cunning man, cunning woman, wise man or wise woman. The journal entry in English in the Llyfr Cyfrin refers to a 'wise man'. The current trend in academia is to refer to the general profession or class of persons who performed these kinds of tasks as service magicians.
3 The modern Welsh witch Mhara Starling refers to herself as 'swynydd'.
4 Kate Bosse-Griffiths, *Byd y Dyn Hysbys* (Y Lolfa, 1977) p. 133. My translation. The rest of her account is worth quoting.
'I wonder where the Dyn Hysbys got hold of the charms/spells to call on the Tylwyth Teg? Why did he write out only one of them in English? That suggests that welsh was originally the language of the other spells, or at least at the stage when the Dyn Hysbys of Denbighshire came across them. Who wrote them first of all, and when? I do not know. But I still have hope of coming across the answer. And this is why: at the stage in which I was about to finish the final typescript of this small book, I had a chat with Professor Cecil Price of the University College Swansea, while speaking first/initially about a new lecturer in his department who was proficient in the art of reading fate–or telling fortunes– through studying the lines of the hand (palm-reading), an art that is associated with gypsies rather than dynion hysbys; going on to

name John Harries, Cwrt-y-cadno, and similar dynion hysbys in Montgomeryshire.
"There are still some available," he said, "and people write to them from every corner of the land for help and advice."
Longstanding Swansea bookseller and Dylan Thomas specialist Jeff Towns recalled Cecil Price on his blog.
'. . . many of my earliest customers came from Swansea University's academic staff, in particular Professor Cecil Price, the head of the English Department. Cecil was a proper bibliophile and I learned much from him. He was a serious collector of Chesterfield and edited Sheridan's plays for publication, but he was also very keen on Welsh Writing in English (which I had begun to specialize in). It was Cecil who had invited Dylan Thomas to speak to Swansea staff and students during which Dylan traded insults with Kingsley Amis. A year or two after Cecil died his books appeared at a Sotheby's auction in London and I bought many good lots including his Dylan Thomas books which included a fine unpublished letter to Cecil from Dylan himself!'
https://www.discoverdylanthomas.com/blog4
When I contacted Jeff Towns, asking whether he had heard anything about the current ownership of either Llyfr Cyfrin or Cecil Price's magical notebook, I received no reply.
5 Her son Heini Gruffydd points out that the town of Wittenberg itself had a long history of anti-Semitism. Martin Luther, its most famous son, held some rabidly anti-Jewish views. Heini Gruffydd, *A Haven From Hitler* (Y Lolfa, 2014) p.32-37.

6 A moving obituary by Marion Löffler, another German scholar who has made her home in Wales, made be found in 'A Tribute to Dr. Kate' in *Minerva transactions of the Royal Institution of South Wales* Vol. 7, 1999 p. 4-7. https://journals.library.wales/view/1225327/1225678/#?m=6
7 In a critical review fellow scholar Morfydd Owen accuses her of a sketchy and superficial analysis and of making sweeping generalisations on the basis of evidence that has not been properly examined.
Morfydd E.Owen, Review of Byd y Dyn Hysbys in *Y Traethodydd* Cyf. CXXXIV, Rhif 570, Ionawr 1979 p.171-172
8 'Ac wedi dysgu "crefft y gwynt" (the trade of wind) am saith mlynedd fel disgybl i Ddynion Hysbys yngh Nghymru, gwelaf fod yr amser wedi dod it ddatgan fy mhrofiad terfynol a syfrdanolo, sef bod cyfyngau anweledig yn gallu cael effeithiau gweladwy, bod Duwdod yn nechreuad popeth a bod ysytyr ym mhopeth.' *Byd y*

Dyn Hysbys p. 133-134.
9 John Gwynedd Griffiths, 'Swyn i atal serch', *Heddiw*, 6, 177-8. 1941 'A Modern Welsh Anti-Love Charm with Ancient Antecedents'. *Anthropos* 60, 108-12. 1965
10 My translation.
11 John Gwynedd Griffiths, 'Swyn i atal serch' ('A Charm to Prevent Love'). Griffiths comments, 'There are signs of this charm of very old elements, although it was given (to the best of my knowledge) by a witch who is now alive. In witchcraft the age of a charm is always a virtue. The direction to make a fire when preparing a charm is very common. Salt also had a great reputation for working wonders. Compare the story told by Evan Isaac (*Coelion Cymru*, 29-30) from Sir John Rhŷs's *Celtic Folklore* about the Fairies stealing a child and abusing it. A charm is made by a gŵr cyfarwydd to restore the child: "He made the man seek a shovel and cover it with salt and cut a cross into it. Then he put the shovel on the fire in the stranger's room, with the window open. the baby was left unattended on the doorstep."'

Llyfr Cyfrin y Dyn Hysbys o Sir Ddinbych

Hunforddied I alw ar yspudion a
Elwir toliwnthiteg..

Rhaid ir lle y boch un galw. arnunt
fod yn bur banweth a Kadach wedi ei
dannu ar lawr neu ar vaws yngulch i
troedfedd oddiwrth y culch neu ur Sircil
ar lawr a bod Cuw i'an neu ddorun ar
all wedi ei rostis yn _____ a _____
dagil wen fechen ai llond o. _____ glan
_____g a haner Peint o Sec _____ _____
a chwart o gwrw da a ffeint o hufen _____
mewn Dergil yr hun fudd yni gunud___
hwnt yn gudnabadd ufach ag yn mwu
Cyffillgar I wnuthur aich Dyminied ur
Pthau hwn Seff yr Dysklau ni chwrddant ar
Culch wrth ei galw mau yn raid aich b__
gwedi _____chi yn lan ag yn hard___

Page 1 of Llyfr Cyfrin

y mawr Calun Dulhy Calch Sudd yn
gwasnaethu yr holl ymadrodd or blaen
ond ymhell waith diachon ganeud fordd
arall os bydd Rhuw Gladdfa neu rinw bethob
arall anaidolfol fod Ch wedi eu wneuthur yn
y lle honno neu ar y lle y bo un Gwedi
gwneud am dano i hun neu Cyfelib ir
ir faith waithred neu lle bo un gwedi
ymaadol ar bud mewn Ceealondeb agu
anyuresttrwudd trwu fod yn wag o fam od
terfunau neu lowburan neu amriw gam
wuthredodd ae sudd yn ain sydd hau
Cwfwinwudder yr aflonnudd ddu eulle
brigian oll y an feltu budd Dunion yn Clowed
yn ynos riw ddieithrol Dychrunillud ag
ofnaduu leisie neis lini au Echrudus mawn
Perthynas ir un rhuw ymau yn Rhaid.

Page 9 of Llyfr Cyfrin

19

a budded tangnefedd dduw Rhinged a mesi ag yr wisg ymoich tynghedi i addasg drwtof Panalionif arun achosun patrud bunay y galwnf a hunnw yn ol Anghiuddiby Hollalluog Amen.

The ten General names whichsoever be, Alihim, Elohe, Zebaoth, Elion, Eferachia, Adonay, Iah, Tetragrammaton, Saday, — Give Commandment O God to thee, Strength Confirm O God thy Work in us let them be as Dust before the face of the wind, and let the Angel of the Lord Scatter them, let all their ways be Darkness and uncertain, and let the Angel of the Lord persecute them part of the 7 and 35 psalm

Page 14 (or 19) of Llyfr Cyfrin

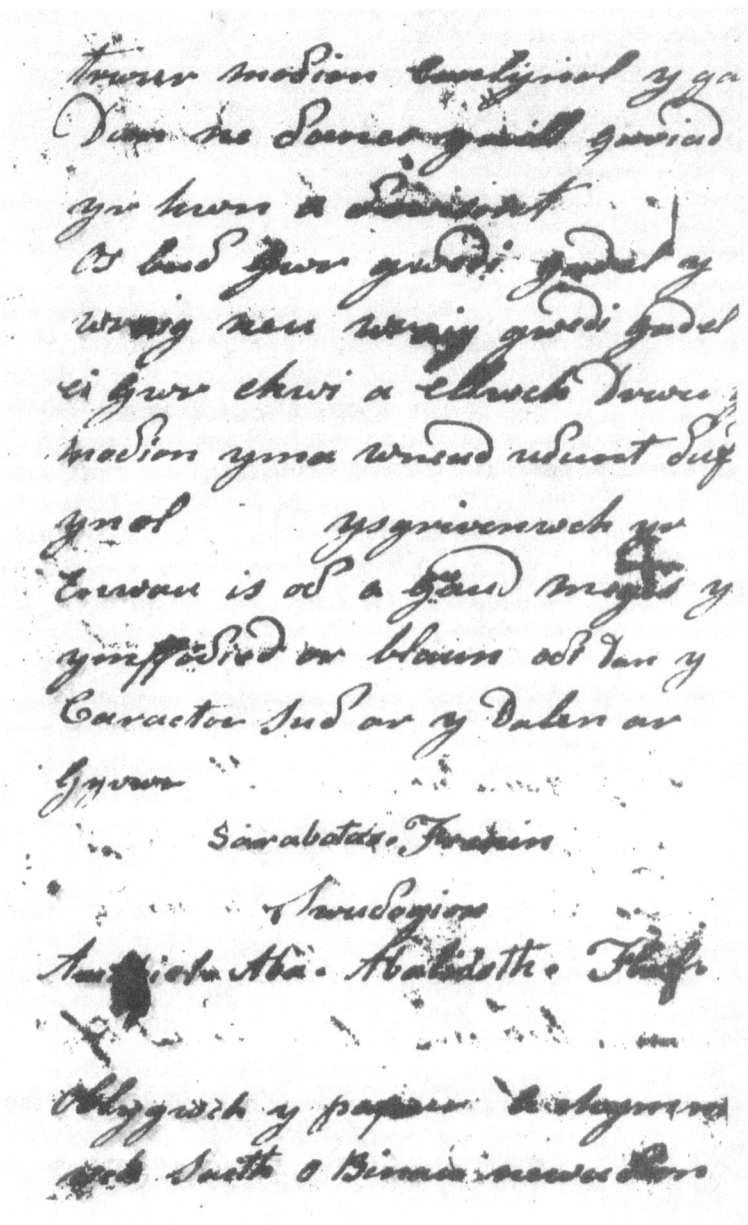

A ffigwch y papur ynna thrwy
Saith waith Drwyddo a gadewch y pin-
yn y pigiad dywetha fel hun yn
arverwch y pinau un bob nos am
Saith noswaith A cadewch y papur
ar pinau yndo hed oni weler
Eich Ewllis oherwydd fe fydd yn effeithio
yn calon dros lawer o amser
Cofiwch eich bod i wneud eich dymuny-
ied at yr ysprydion bob nos ar
iddynt gyflawni Eich Dymuniad
ag ar ol cal ych Dymuniad towlwch
y papur ir tan ar pinau hefyd

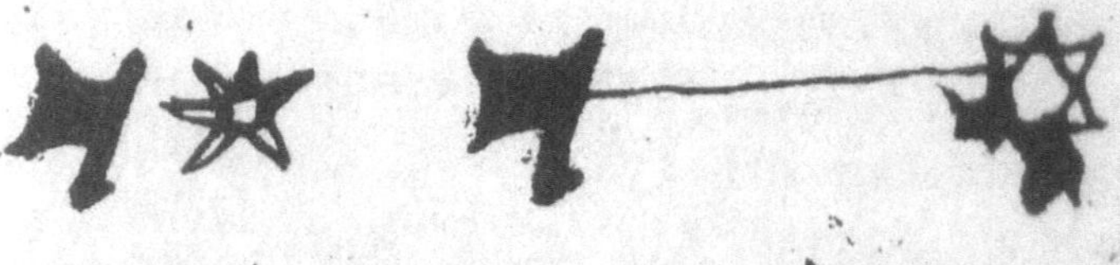

the Angels of Friday Anael Rachiel Sachiel

Page 26 of Llyfr Cyfrin

Kate Bosse-Griffiths tells us, 'There is also a page noting the contents – but not all the contents.' The following contents is extracted from her references and index in *Byd y Dyn Hysbys*.

1 Daergoel Geomancy
2 Daergoel Geomancy
1-3 Hyfforddiad i alw ar yr ysbrydion a elwir tylwyth teg
4-5 To Conjure the Spirits commonly called Fairies
5-6 Sator Arepo
8-10, 12-13 Hyfforddiad i alw ar yr ysbrydion a elwir tylwyth teg
14 ffigur swyn
19 The ten general names of God
20-1 Daergoel Geomancy
22 Certain General Aphorisms
41-42 a method "To cure witchcraft" that has been quoted from the Blackgrave MSS
84-5 The moon in Aries, life is long
115 A legendary charm used in former days in gathering herbs
117 To invocate and converse with the spirit of the dead
122-3 Another strange necromantic spell.
123-5 In the power of God I walk on my way
137-9 Daergoel Geomancy
140 Thus Words being spoke with great reverence
143-4 Upon Oct. 25, 1832.
145-6 Daergoel Geomancy
185-6 A request to the spirits if a man has left his wife
Free page olwyn swyn magic wheel

What follows is the text of Llyfr Cyfrin y Dyn Hysbys o Sir Ddinbych to the extent to which it can be reconstructed from Kate Bosse-Griffiths' quotations in *Byd y Dyn Hysbys* and the few photographs reproduced on the previous pages. Her comments have been included in the main text here when she describes parts of Llyfr Cyfrin that she does not quote directly. Extensive notes follow the text, including many of the complete sources which have been copied into the notebook.

1-3 **Hyfforddiad i alw ar yr ysbrydion a elwir tylwyth teg**

Rhaid i'r lle y boch yn galw arnynt fod yn bur lanwedd a chadach wedi ei daenu ar lawr neu ar fwrdd yn gylch i droedfedd oddi wrth y cylch neu y sircil ar lawr; a bod cyw iâr neu ryw aderyn arall wedi ei rostio yn daclus a chawg neu ddysgl wen fechan a'i llond o ddŵr glân rhedegog a hanner peint o hufen llaeth mewn dysgl. Yr hyn fydd yn gwneud hwynt yn gydnabyddusach ac yn fwy cyfeillgar i wneuthur eich dymuniad.

Y pethau hyn, sef y dysglau, ni chwrddant â'r cylch. Wrth eu galw mae yn rhaid eich bod wedi ymolchyd yn lân ac yn hardd.[1]

An Instruction for Calling Upon the Spirits Called the Tylwyth Teg

The place where you call upon them must be very clean and a cloth should be spread out on the ground or on a table about a foot from the circle or ring on the ground; and a nicely roasted chicken or other bird and a bowl or small white dish full of pure running water and half a pint of cream in a dish.

This will make them more familiar and more amenable to doing your will.

These things, that is, the dishes, should not touch the circle. When calling upon them you must have washed yourself so to be clean and pleasant.

Eisteddwch wrth fwrdd neu ryw le arall a rhowch drosto gadach gwyn golau yn crogi droedfedd dros y bwrdd; ac yna galwch ar yr ysbydion sydd wedi eu gosod yn bennaf ar lywodraethu ar y lleill, y rhai a elwir Meiob ac Oberion.

A gan y rhain y mae saith chwaer sef Sibia, Reflilia, Forta, Folla, Affrita, Julia, Benula. I'r rhain sydd eto llawer lleng o ysbrydion gwasanaethgar yn wandro yma a thraw a ganddynt gadwedigaeth ar drysor cuddiedig.

A thry'r cyfarwyddyd uchod fe ellid eu cael allan ond galw fel y mae yn canlyn. Galw ar yr ysbrydion ynghyd: "Yr wyf i yn eich tynghedu ac yn gorchymyn ichwi ysbrydion daearol y rhai sydd bennaf yn llywodraethu ar y tylwyth teg sef Miscob ag Oberion yn enw yr Hollalluog dduw Jehova a'i unig anedig fab Iese Grist etc.

Yn ganlynol y modd i reoli y rhagddywedig ysbrydion: 'Rwyf yn galw ac yn taer ddeisydu ar ichwi ysbrydion Meicob ag Oberion orchymyn i'r saith chwaer Sibia, Reflilia, Fora, Folla, Offrita, Julia, Benulia y rhai hyn i ymddangos yn eglur mewn mwyneidd-dra ac ewyllys da neu yrru rhyw un o'ch llywodraeth chwi i'n dyheu ac i'n hamddiffyn yn ein Dumuniad yr hyn beth a allant. Yn yr hyn yr wyf yn hyderu ac yn erfyn ac yn ymbil fel yr ydych chwi yn weision i'r goruchaf. . ."[2]

Sit by a table or somewhere else and place over it a light white cloth, draped over the table, and then call upon the spirits which are ranked chief to govern the others, those named Meiob and Oberion.

And the others are seven sisters, that is, Sibia, Reflilia, Fora, Folla, Offrita, Julia, Benula. These also have many legions of serving spirits wandering here and there, and who have guardianship of hidden treasure.

And through the above guidance they may be discovered, but call upon them as follows. Call upon the spirits together, 'I adjure you and command you, earthly spirits by those who are chief in governing over the Tylwyth Teg, that is, Miscob and Oberion, in the name of the Almighty god Jehovah and his only begotten son Jesus Christ, etc.

The way to control the aforementioned spirits is as follows:

'I call upon and fervently beseech you spirits Meicob and Oberion to command the seven sisters Sibia, Reflilia, Fora, Folla, Offrita, Julia, Benulia to manifest clearly in kindness and good will or to send someone under your authority to our desiring and defend us in our wish as they are able. In this I trust and beseech and implore you as servants to the supreme Most High. . .'

4-5 To Conjure the Spirits commonly called Fairies

First you must have a square cristal or Venice glass of three inches square. Lay that glass or cristal in the blood of a white hen three Wednesdays or three Fridays. Then take it out and wash it with holy water. Then take three hazel wands upon one side and write the spirits' name on the wand and calling the spirit three times by its name conjuring it to make its appearance unto you at the day and hour, naming the time. This you are to do with each wand separately.

Then bury the wands in the earth under some pleasant hill where they are most likely to hound upon Wednesdays. And on Friday following take them up and call her to appearance. In conjuring her in the usual way.

And if the spirit do not make its appearance at the first call you should continue until nine times, waiting a little between each time.

And the spirit will appear at the ninth call if not sooner. Then you bind the spirit in the usual way for to appear in that glass or cristal at any time when you call upon it.

The best time to do this is the moon increasing and in good aspect with Venus or Mercury or both. The hours of calling are at eight, then or three and those are the best hours to call the spirit to the glass at any time after which you have no need to use cantation.[3]

5-6 Sator Arepo

Chwi a ellwch alw amryw chwiorydd fel y mae yn canlyn: SATOR AREPO TENET OPERA ROTAS ....'

(No translation)

You can call several sisters as follows:
SATOR AREPO TENET OPERA ROTAS

8-10 **Hyfforddiad i alw ar yr ysbrydion a elwir tylwyth teg**

... gadewir i'r ysbryd neu i'r ysbrydion sydd yn cadw yr lle gael eu rhyddhau yn fuan mewn heddwch a thangnefedd, yr hyn sydd yn erfynedig ac yn blaen â: 'Thangnefydd Duw yn wastad a daioni rhyngoch chwi a minnau. Gwenewch imi fel gweision i'r goruchaf.' Felly y rhai cyntaf hyn sydd i'w harferyd y saith noswaith o gynyddiad y lleuad, a dechrau ar yr wythfed nos, sef y nesaf ar ôl i'r lleuad newid. Ac ar yr wythfed rhaid galw naw gwaith yn yr awr a dechrau unarddeg o'r gloch am eu bod hwy yn arferol ymddangos at yr amser hwnnw ac fe allant basio mewn terfynau heb gennad.[4]

An Instruction for Calling Upon the Spirits Called the Tylwyth Teg

Allow the spirit or spirits that keep the place to have their freedom soon in peace and tranquillity, which is implored and go on with, 'God's peace always and goodness between you and me. Make me as a servant to the Almighty.' So the first thing is to employ it for seven nights of the waxing moon, and to start on the eighth night, that is, the next after the new moon. And on the eighth you must call nine times in the hour that begins at eleven o'clock in which they usually appear towards this time and they can pass in boundaries without leave.

12 **Hyfforddiad i alw ar yr ysbrydion a elwir tylwyth teg**

Y mae'n canlyn dull y cylch sydd yn gwasanaethu yr holl ymadrodd o'r blaen. Ond ambell waith dichon gwneud ffordd arall.

Os bydd rhyw laddfa, neu ryw bechod arall anneddfol fod wedi ei wneuthr yn y lle hwnnw, neu ar y lle y bo un wedi ymwneud amdano ei hun neu'r cyffelybion i'r fath weithred; neu lle bo un wedi ymadael â'r byd mewn creulondeb ac anonestrwydd trwy fod yn euog o symud terfynau neu lwybrau neu amryw gamweithredoedd ac sydd yn anufuddhau cyfiawnder – yn aflonyddu ei le trigiannol, gan felly bydd dynion yn clywed yn y nos ryw ddiethrol ddychrynllyd ac ofnadwy leisiau neu luniau echrydus mewn perthynas i'r un rhyw, y mae'n rhaid bod yn gryf ac yn ffyddlon ac yn ddyfal weddio am nerth i beri iddynt siarad ac i eglurhau eu achos a'u trwbleth. Diau fod yr ysbrydion hun, sef y Tylwyth Teg, yn fwy daearol a chymdeithasol iddynt na rhai uffernol ac wybrennol. O achos hwn i gyd addefont yn gweneuthur gwaith yn rhith crefftwyr yn lladrata brin arian ac aur ac yn cymryd o'r mwyn yn y wlad lle mae nhw yn cyffredin weithio yn enwedig mewn hen waith plwmbo...[5]

An Instruction for Calling Upon the Spirits Called the Tylwyth Teg

There follows a form of the circle which serves the entire previous statement. But sometimes it is possible to do it another way.

If some slaughter or some other unlawful sin has been inflicted in that place, or at the place where someone had done away with himself, or things similar to this sort of act; or in a place where someone had departed the world in cruelty and dishonesty through being guilty of moving boundaries or paths or any sort of transgression and which disobeys righteousness–disturbing its dwelling place, by such will men hear in the night some strange, dreadful and awful voice or frightful shout in relation to someone, there has to be strong and faithful and diligent praying for the power to make them speak and to clarify their purpose and their trouble. It is certain that these spirits, that is, the Tylwyth Teg, are more earthly and sociable than those infernal and celestial.

Because of this they dwell together doing work in the guise of craftsmen stealing rare silver and gold and taking from the minerals in the land where they commonly work famously in an old lead mine.

13 Ffordd arall o alw ar yr ysbrydion a elwir Tylwyth Teg ac i gael allan drysor cuddiedig.

Mewn ystafell ddirgelaidd o oleuwch ac ynddi arogl peraidd, y mae'n gymwys gweneud y gwaith hwn sef ysgrifennu â gwaed y ceiliog du ar bapur gwan glân yn gyntaf eich deisyfiad fel y mae yn canlyn:

Sathan Barampar Barbarson, Dewch ataf fi mewn prysurdeb i'r lle hwn. Dygwch imi y trysor i'r fan a'r lle yma.Yna enwch y fan lle y mae eich amheuaeth fod trysor yn guddiedig. Yna bydded y cylch yn barod gennych ar lawr y stafell a chwmpawd wrth ei gonglau ddal ar lawr yn glos a phegiau ynddynt fel y gallant fod yn sad. Pan eloch i mewn i'r ystafell gosodwch eich deisyfed sy wedi sgrifennu â gwaed y ceiliog du ar y drws a'r sircel ar lawr a galw yn y pen arall i'r ystafell yng ngolwg y drws a'r nos yn serog-olau dawel. Dull y sircel neu'r pedwar ongliad sydd fel hyn.

I wneud y sircel hon rhaid pisio pedwar pasmant at ei gilydd neu groen llo. Rhaid iddynt fod yn sgwâr ac yn llyfn a'r sgrifen arno sef y modd y dangosir yn yr arwyddocâd sydd tu arall i'r ddalen yn batrwm. Ac yno hi a fydd yn gyfleus i'w chario i'r fan a fynnoch. Ac y mae yn fwy cymwys nag un wedi ei gwneud ar lawr os bydd y sircel wedi ei gwneud y modd yma. Rhaid i chwi gymryd sugungold Mair i olchi yr enwau sydd tu mewn i'r sircel a'r enwau sydd tu allan â gwaed y ceiliog du.[6]

Another way of calling upon the spirits called the Tylwyth Teg and to discover hidden treasure.

In a room hidden from light and a sweet odour in it, it is suitable to do this work, that is, first to write your desire with the blood of a black cockerel on clean blank paper as follows:

Sathan Barampar Barbarson, Come to me in haste to this place. Bring me the treasure to this place and location. Then name the place where your suspicion is that treasure is hidden. Then let the circle be ready for you on the floor of the room and hold down the circle by its corners closely with pegs in it so they are firm. When you go into the room place your desire that is written in the blood of a black cockerel on the door and place the circle down and call from the other end of the room in sight of the door and the quiet starlit night. The form of the circle or the four corners is as so.

To make this circle it is necessary to put four parchments or calfskins together. They must be square and smooth with the writing on them, that is the way shown in the invocation that is on the other side of the page as a pattern. And then it will be convenient to carry to the place you wish. And there it will be more suitable than one has made on a floor if the circle will have been made this way.

You must take marigold juice to wash the names that are within the circle and the names that are outside with black cockerel's blood.

14 **ffigur swyn**[7]

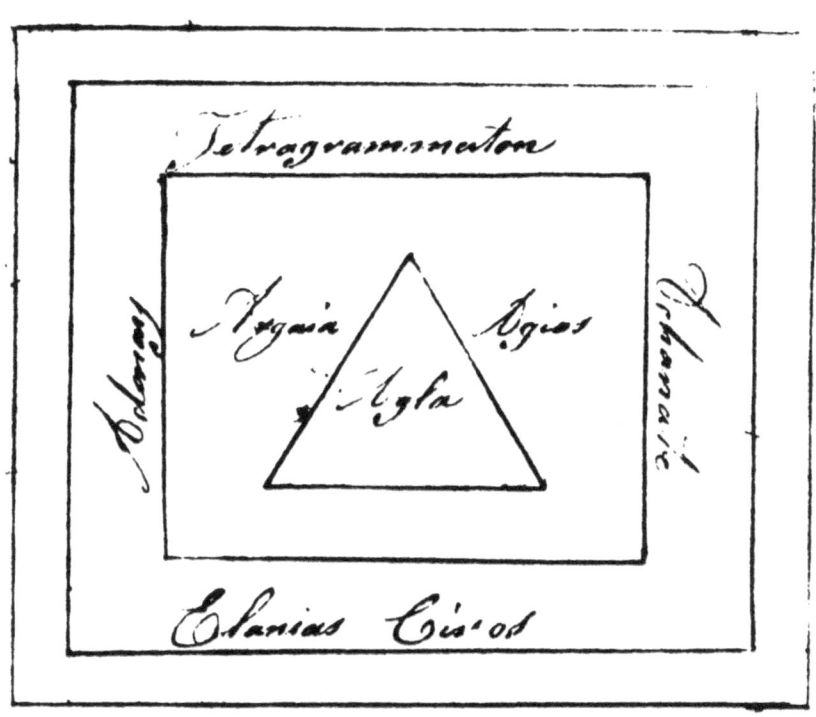

A Magical Figure

19 The ten general names of God

A bydded tangnefedd Dduw rhyngoch a myfi ag yr wyf yn eich tynghedi i ddyfod ataf pan alwaf ar un achosion pa bryd bynag y galwaf a hwnnw yn ol arglwyddiaeth yr hollalluog Amen.[8]

'The ten general names (of God) which are El, Elohim, Elsha, Zabaoth, Elion, Essurehie, Adonay, Iah, Tetragrammaton, Sadday'

Give commandment O God to thee, strength

Confirm O God thy work in us let them be as Dust before the face of the wind, and let the Angels of the Lord scatter them, let all them aye the Darkness and uncertainty and let the Angel of the Lord persecute them part of the 7 and 35 psalms[9]

And may the peace of God be between you and me and I adjure you to come when I call for whatever reasons I call and this according to the dominion of the Almighty. Amen.

22 Certain General Aphorisms

'Choice Aphorismes of Cardans seven segements by William Lillee-Englished and disposed under proper titles. Certain general aphorismes to be observed by the Artists.'

Certain general aphorismes to be observed by the Artist: 1rst: Life is short, art long. Experience not easily obtained, judgment difficult and therefore 'tis necessary that a Student not only exercises himself in considering several figures, but also that he diligently read the writings of others who have treated rationally of this Science, and make it his business to find out the true natural causes of things by Experiments; to know the certain places and possessions of the planets, fixed stars and constellations, but above all to be a passionate lover of truth...[10]

See notes for the full text of the Aphorisms of Cardan.

41-42

Kate Bosse-Griffiths: 'ar dudalen 41-2 nodir bod hyfforddiant "To cure witchcraft" wedi ei dyfynnu o "Blackgrave MSS'

84-5 **The moon in Aries, life is long**

The Moon in Aries, life is long,
In Taurus, Gemini, Cancer: strong.
But when the Moon in Leo strives,
Full short and painful are men's lives.

In Virgo, thou wilt behold her true,
Happy and Just, and amorous too.
But still men's years are short and few.

Then view her swift, through Libra speed,
The vital flame shall constant feed
And famous make in art and deed.

Wail, when the Scorpio persues
The Sagittarius.Arrow, thews
And sinews potent grace this letter sign.

Long life and happy then is thine.
In Capricornus, in Aquarius scant,
But Pisces constant wards the fatal dent.[11]

Kate Bosse-Griffiths: 'on p. 41-42 is noted a method "To cure witchcraft" that has been quoted from the Blackgrave MSS.'

115

Kate Bosse Griffiths: 'ar dudalen 115 dyfynnir "A legendary charm used in former days in gathering herbs" gan nodi "taken from an old black letter missal in possession of the mercary".'

Kate Bosse-Griffiths: 'on p. 115 is quoted "A legendary charm used in former days in gathering herbs" with a note, "taken from an old black letter missal in possession of the mercary".'[12]

117 **To invocate and converse with the spirit of the dead**

I do take the earth in which thou must enter into, that thy spirit may come into the church to speak unto me and fulfil my will, and that it never shall have the power to rest or be quiet until thou come to speak with me and fulfil my will and commandment.

Bosse-Griffiths: 'Wedi ynganu'r geiriau rhybuddol, rhaid mynd i'r eglwys gan ddal i gadw'r pridd yn y llaw ac aros hyd nes i'r corff gael ei gludo i fwen i'r eglwys, "and thou shalt see a twofold spirit coming and the spirit of the dead like cats."

Wrth weld ysbryd y dyn marw yn yr eglwys rhaid adrodd enwau Duw. Ar ôl gwasanaeth rhaid dilyn y cynhebrwng hyd at y bedd, ac arosi'r corff gael ei ostwng i'r bedd gwag. Ac wedi i bawb arall fynd i ffwrdd, fe fydd yr ysbryd yn dod. Nid oes raid ofni, ni all wneud unrhyw niwed. Ond yr awr galwer ar y dyn marw wrth ei enw, gan ddweud fel a canlyn:'

Bosse-Griffiths: 'After pronouncing the warning words, you must go to church and take the soil in hand and wait until the body is transported to the church, "and thou shalt see a twofold spirit coming and the spirit of the dead like cats." Seeing the spirit of the dead man in the church requires reciting the names of God. After the service the funeral must be followed to the grave, and the body waiting to be reduced to the empty grave. And when everyone else is gone, the spirit will come. There is no need to be afraid, it can do no harm. But now call upon the dead man by his name, saying as follows:'

117 **Continued**

O N, I do conjure thee by the passion of our Lord Jesus Christ,
And by the virgin nature of the sweet Mary,
And by the twelve apostles,
And by the four evangelists,
And by all the martyrs and confessors,
And by the earth which I have in my hand
Which is of the earth wherein thy body is buried in,

And by the constellations of heaven,
And by all the virtues and powers which are in heaven and on earth,
And by all the angels and their fall in which is the cause of man's creation,
And by the words which Christ spake as he hung upon the altar of the cross,
That is Ely, Ely Lama Zabachthani semiforas [sic],
That thou do not offend me by any manners of lying or deceit,
But that you declare the truth of all things when I do call thee by thy name, o N.,
And in answering me truly with an understanding voice,
And the true tongue and speech which I do understand.

And I do bind thee,
And I conjure thee by all the words aforesaid,
And I command thee by our Lord Jesus XT
And by his most precious blood,
And by him that will come to judge the quick and the dead
And the world by fire.
Amen.[13]

(No translation)

122-3 **Another strange necromantic spell.'from a curious manuscript**

Bosse-Griffiths: 'Fe roddir yn yr un llyfr Cyfrin hyfforddiant haws ei ddilyn o dan y pennawd "Another strange necromantic spell.". Yno conghorir unrhyw un sydd eisiau annerch neu gwrdd â pherson marw (neu fyw), i fynd i'r fynwent, ar nos Wener, rhwng naw a deg o'r gloch, a cherdded o amgylch saith waith. Ac wedi iddo ddod i'r gornel, rhaid sefyll yn stond ac adrodd gweddi'r Arglwydd a'r Credo, "and before you have gone seven times around, you shall meet them you would meet with all personality as they were want to go."'[14]

Bosse-Griffiths: 'The same secret book gives an easier-to-follow instruction under the heading "Another strange necromantic spell." There, anyone who wishes to address or meet a dead (or living) person, is advised to go to the cemetery, on a Friday night, between nine and ten o'clock, and walk around it seven times. And when coming to the corner, you must stand and recite the Lord's Prayer and the Creed "and before you have gone seven times around, you shall meet them you would meet with all personality as they were want to go."'[15]

123-5 **In the power of God I walk on my way**

In the power of God, I walk on my way
In the meekness of Christ.

What thieves soever I meet
The Holy Ghost today shall me keep.
Whether I sit or stand, walk or sleep,
The shining of the sun also the brightness of his
  beams shall me help.

The faith of Isaac today shall me lead
The suffering of Jacob today be my speed.
The devotion of the holy Lamb thieves shall let,
The strength of Jesus blessed passion them beset.

The dread of death hold thieves low
The wisdom of Solomon prove their overthrow.
The suffering of Job set them in hold
The chastity of Daniel let what they would.
The speech of Isaac their speech shall spill,
The languishing faith of Ioram let them of their will.

The flaming fires of hell to hit them I bequeath,
The deepness of the deep sea, their hearts to let.

The light of Heaven against them shall rise
The dread of serpents cause their hearts to grieve.

The help of Heaven cause thieves to stand
He that made the Sun and Moon bind them with his
  hand
As sure as St. Bartholomew bound the fiend with
  hair of his beard.[16]

(No translation)

140 **Thus Words being spoke with great reverence**

Thus Words being spoke with great revarens and faith has Don wonders[17]

143-4 Hanesyn am ddadreibio 10

Upon Oct. 25, 1832.
A farmer from the parish of Hope, Flintshire, met with me in Wrexham. And complained much that his cattle and milk had been witched. And that some of the cattle had lost their dids. I asked him how long had it being [sic] so. He told me between two and three months and his loss was very great, and that all his cheese were spoilt. And I asked whether he had not being with anyone else trying to get cured. And he told me that his son had being seven times with a wise man that was called Shon y rhose but no better and that he could not do the work three moons, and I persuaded that I should be cured in that time.

Therefore I was persuaded to go to one W. Allwood, a gentleman farmer near hope. And he ordered me to comply to you. And I hope that you will endavour to bring me out of the ruinous concern.

And I promised him that I would without delay. Accordingly I did through God's assistance to the great astonishment and satisfaction of the Farmer and his family. For they told me that the first cheese that was made after was richer and better than could be expected.[18]

An account of unwitching

185-6 Deisyfiad ar yr ysbrydion os bydd gŵr wedi gadael y wraig

Trwy'r moddion canlynol y gall dyn neu ddynes ennill gariad yr hwn a ddewisont.

Os bydd gŵr wedi gadael y wraig neu wraig wedi gadael ei gŵr, chwi a ellwch drwy'r moddion yma wneud iddynt ddyfod yn ôl. Ysgrifennwch yr enwau isod â gwaed megis y hyffordied o'r blaen oddi dan y caracter sydd ar y dalen ar gyfer

Sarabotas, Frenin
Swyddogion
Amabiel. Aba. Abalidoth. Flad.

Plygwch y papur a chymerwch saith o binnau newyddion.

A phigwch y papur yma a thraw Saith waith drwyddo a gadewch y pin yn y pigiad diwethaf. Fel hyn ymarferwch y pinnau un bob nos am saith noswaith. A chadwch y papur a'r pinnau ynddo hyd oni wnelir Eich Ewyllys. Oherwydd fe fydd yr effaith yn canlyn dros lawer o amser.

Cofiwch eich bod i wneud eich deisyfiad at yr ysbrydion bob nos ar iddynt gwplhau Eich dymuniad. Ag ar ôl cael eich dymuniad twlwch y papur i'r tân a'r pinnau hefyd.[19]

The angels of Friday: Anael, Rachiel, Sachiel.

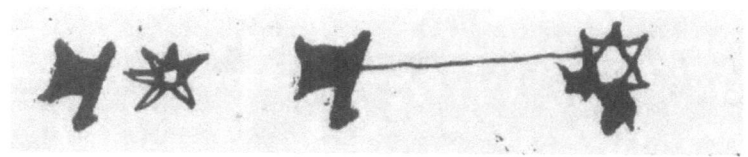

A request to the spirits if a man has left his wife

Through the following methods a man or woman can can win the love they have chosen. If a man has left his wife or a woman has left her husband you can make them come back through these methods. Write the names below in blood as per the method previously given below the character that is on the page for

Sarabotas, king
Officers
Amabiel. Aba. Abalidoth. Flad.
Fold the paper and take seven new pins.
Pierce the paper seven times here and there and keep the pin in the last hole. Practise with the pins in this way once every night for seven nights. And keep the paper and the pins in it until you see your desire. For the result will follow after many attempts.

Remember to make your supplication to the spirits every night for them to complete your wish. And after getting your wish fling the paper into the fire with the pins also.

58 Pages From a Welsh Cunning Man's Book

Tudalen rhydd olwyn swyn

This Figuar among the Ancients was considered a Greate preservation against the Enemies. And they say who so ever weareth the Figuar need Fear no Foe.[20]

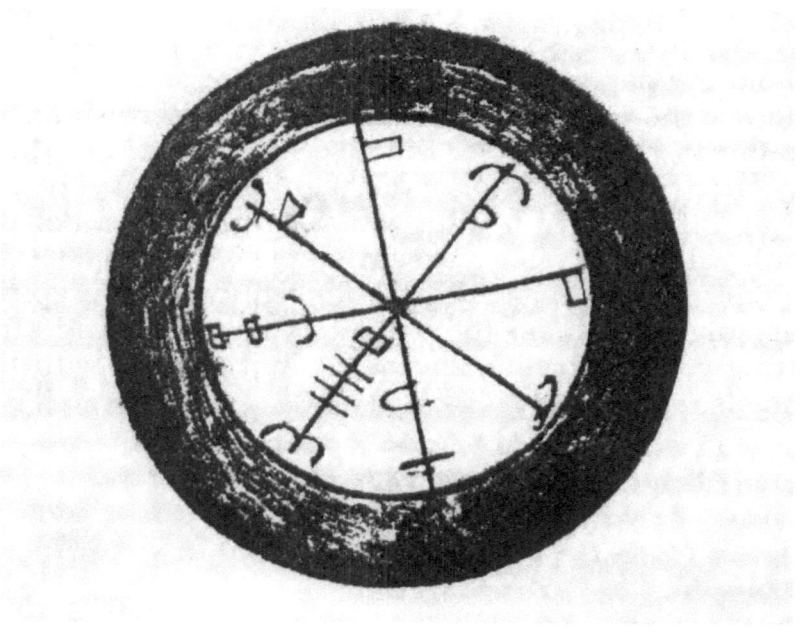

Empty Page, Magic Wheel

Scot Book XV Chap 7: 'Who so beareth this signe about him, all spirits shall doo him homage.' and 'Who so beareth this signe about him, let him feare no fo, but feare GOD.'

Notes

1 The opening spell is discussed in detail in the chapter 'The Seven Sisters Spell'.

2 Bosse-Griffiths adds, 'After preparing for the spirits, it is instructed how to behave and also the names of the spirits are given and how to summon them and to release them afterwards.'

3 This is in English and is very similar to Bodleian MS. Ashmole 1406, 'An excellent way to gett a Fayrie,' up to the mention of Friday, after which the texts diverge considerably. The Llyfr Cyfrin version focuses on scrying the spirit in the glass and binding it, whereas the Bodleian spell goes on to describe the making of an eye unguent, presumably for seeing fairies. This may be a separate spell which has been appended to the text.

'First, get a broad square christall or Venice glasse, in length and breadth three inches. Then lay that glasse or christall in the blood of a white henne, three Wednesdayes or three Fridayes. Then take it out and wash it with holy aqua water, and fumigate it. Then take three hazle sticks, or wands, of an yeare groth; pill peel them fayre and white; and make them soe longe as you write the spiritt's name, or fayrie's name, which you call three times on every stick being made flatt on one side. Then bury them under some hill, whereat you suppose fayries haunt, the Wednesday before you call her: and the Friday followinge take them uppe and call her at eight, or three, or ten of the clocke, which be good planetts and houres for that turne; but when you call be in cleane life and turne thy face towards the East, and when you have her bind her in that stone and glasse.'

See also Daniel Harms, *Of Angels, Demons and Spirits* (Llewellyn, 2019) p.290.

'An Excellent Way to Get a Fairy' was also included in Hockley's 1829 *Occult Spells*. The editor of the Teitan edition comments 'The original conjuration was included in a collection of alchemical papers, then housed in the Ashmolean Museum at Oxford, and now at the Bodleian (8259, 1406, 2). Hockley may have had access to these, or he may have relied on the version published in Thomas Percy, Bishop of Dromore, *Reliques of Ancient English Poetry* (London: J. Dodsley, 1765), Vol. III, p. 267, a work that was well-known to antiquaries.' p.8

Llyfr Cyfrin recommends the timing be when the moon is increasing and there is a good aspect with Venus and Mercury whereas Bodleian suggests summoning 'hir at 8 or 3 or 10 of the clocke which be good plannetts and howres for that turne:'
The Sator Arepo formula is also part of the same seven sisters spell. The oldest extant example of the SATOR square is found in Pompei and many others have been found carved in stone. The letters may be rearranged to spell out PATER NOSTER, 'Our Father' but the use of the squares predates Christianity. SATOR AREPO squares have a long history of use in Britain. No early material examples survive in Wales but a potsherd found in the 1970s in the Manchester area dates to the late second century, and one found in Cirencester in 1868 to a similar time.

S	A	T	O	R
A	R	E	P	O
T	E	N	E	T
O	P	E	R	A
R	O	T	A	S

The SATOR square is often found in magical manuscripts, and in charms, usually written out as a phrase rather than arranged as a square.
A sixteenth century Welsh manuscript (Wellcome MS 417, f. 50v.) contains a charm against a cough which instructs the user to take an inch of an elder rod, hollow it out and carve SATOR AREPO TENET OPERA ROTAS in evry corner of five squares along the ring. The patient must then drink water from it and tie it around his neck.
Marie Trevelyan in her 1909 book *Folk-Lore and Folk-Stories of Wales* writes,
'An amulet used for defeating evil spirits even more than sickness and infection ran as follows : "Rotas, Opera, Tenet, Arepo, Sator." This was seen inscribed on a small stone in the year 1850 in Glamorgan, but the person who copied the inscription was not allowed by the owner to keep this ancient relic. What became of it subsequently is not known. It was probably found among Roman remains, or with Roman coins, and used by a Romanized Welsh person, for a British torque was found near it.'
Kate's husband Gwyn wrote an article on the word 'Arepo, see J. Gwyn Griffiths, '"Arepo" in the Magic "Sator" Square' The

4 This is also part of the seven sisters spell. Either the spell was interrupted in the notebook by the spell 'To Conjure the Spirits' or, more likely, Kate Bosse-Griffiths has mistaken the order.

5 The first sentence is part of the previous spell, the seven sisters.

The circle referred to must be that of *The Book of Treasure Spirits* 114. The copy from Testunau Swyngyfaredd is reproduced on the next page.

The next passage loosely resembles the section 'Of Types of Treasure & Hauntings' that is found in MS Sloane 3824 (*The Book of Treasure Spirits* p.116) between the Seven Sisters spell and the Sarabotas spell, both of which are found in Llyfr Cyfrin.

These are liminal places. The spooky implications of a location where someone has been killed or someone has committed suicide are obvious, but potentially as liminal, and rather poetic, are places where a boundary or a footpath has been moved. Moving a property boundary or diverting or blocking off a footpath would have been as contentious and anti-social then as it is nowadays. There are biblical references to moving boundaries, typically translated as 'boundary stones' or 'landmarks' in English Bibles but just as 'terfynau', 'boundaries' in Welsh. e.g. Job 24:2 Y mae rhai yn symmudo terfynau. (There are people who remove the landmarks.)

Compare *The Book of Treasure Spirits* passage:
'We must understand, that the two last Kind of Terrestrial Spirits, next fore spoken of, being more humane & Courteous to man, than the Aerial & infernals, by reason of their Sympathy & proximity with him, can & do work, & amongst the rest of their Arts they use, to Coin the Gold and Silver they take out of mines, Into that Country's Coin where they find It, and willingly Dwell & frequent in, which is wherein all places where minerals are (for they love not all places, though their mines Be never So Rich and Royal &c) neither where they are, Do they take away or work upon all, but only a small proportion thereof, So, that still getting a little from Every place, as it groweth & Cometh to maturity, always add to their Store.
Some others Delight to wander & go abroad, & work amongst miners, who also bring home their wages. . .'

Rankine, *The Book of Treasure Spirits* p.117
The old lead mine mentioned at the end refers to a particular tradition of the Tylwyth Teg in Cardiganshire. Lewis Morris, a correspondent of the Gentleman's Magazine in 1754, described how, before Esgair y Mwyn lead mine near Pontrhydfendigaid in Cardiganshire was discovered, the local fairies had been observed (and heard) by many people to be hard at work, both day and night. When the mine was established in 1751, though, they disappeared. The same was also the case at Llwyn Llwyd lead mine near Ysbyty Ystwyth, not far from Esgair y Mwyn. (See the following for further examples https://britishfairies.wordpress.com/2019/03/24/the-swart-fairy-of-the-mine-industrial-elves/)
I reproduce the passage in full:
People who know very little of arts or sciences, or the power of Nature (which, in other words, are the powers of the Author of Nature), being full of conceit of their own abilities and knowledge, will laugh at us Cardiganshire miners, who maintain the existence of Knockers in mines, a kind of good-natured impalpable people, but to be seen and heard, and who seem to us to work in the mines; that is to say, they are types, or forerunners, of working in mines, as dreams are of some accidents which happen to us. The barometer falls before rain and storms. If we did not know the construction of it, we should call it a kind of a dream that foretells rain; but we know it is natural, and produced by natural means comprehended by us. Now, how are we sure, or anybody sure, but that our dreams are produced by the same kind of natural means? There is some faint resemblance of this in the sense of hearing; the bird is killed before we hear the report of the gun. However this is, I must speak well of these Knockers, for they have actually stood my very good friends, whether they are aerial beings called spirits, or whether they are a people made of matter not to be felt by our gross bodies, as air and fire and the like. Before the discovery of Esgair y Mwyn mine, these little people (as we call them here) worked hard there day and night; and there are abundance of honest sober people who have heard them, and some persons who have no notion of them or of mines either; but, after the discovery of the great ore, they were heard no more. When I began at Llwyn Llwyd, they worked so fresh there for a considerable time, that they even frightened some young workmen out of the work. This was when we were driving levels, and before we had got any ore; but, when we came to the ore, then they gave over,

and I heard no more talk of them. Our old miners are no more concerned at hearing them blasting, boring holes, landing deads, etc., than if they were some of their own people; and a single miner will stay in the work, in the dead of night, without any man near him, and never think of any fear or harm that they will do him; for, they have a notion that the knockers are of their own tribe and profession, and are a harmless people who mean well. Three or four miners together shall hear them sometimes; but, if the miners stop to take notice of them, the Knockers will also stop; but, let the miners go on at their own work, suppose it is boring, the Knockers will go on as brisk as can be in landing, blasting, or beating down the loose; and they were always heard a little from them before they came to ore. These are odd assertions, but they are certainly facts, though we cannot and do not pretend to account for them. We have now very good ore at Llwyn Llwyd, where the Knockers were heard to work, but have now yielded up the place, and are no more heard. Let who will laugh, we have the greatest reason to rejoice, and thank the Knockers, or rather God, who sends us these notices.
'Lewis Morris, Seq., to His Brother' in *A Selection of Curious Articles from the Gentleman's Magazine: I. Letters to and from eminent persons. II. Miscellaneous articles, including anecdotes of extraordinary persons, useful projects and inventions, &c.* (Longman, Hurst, Rees, and Orme; and J. Munday, 1809), p. 216 https://archive.org/stream/gentlemansmagazi03gommuoft/gentlemansmagazi03gommuoft_djvu.txt

6 This spell follows the previous passage in *Book of Treasure Spirits*. Here it is taken to refer to the Tylwyth Teg, but fairies are not mentioned in the *Book of Treasure Spirits* version, just spirits. It is a treasure hunting spell, titled 'Choice Experiment How to Obtain Treasure Trove.' Llyfr Dewiniaeth also has this spell but doesn't link it to the Tylwyth Teg. Ditto for the almost identical version in Testunau Swyngyfaredd. It seems reasonable to conclude that the author of Llyfr Cyfrin took this to be a way of calling on the Tylwyth Teg for his purposes, despite the arguably more sinister spirits that are referred to in the spell.
Kate Bosse-Griffiths names this 'The Way of the Black Cockerel' and interprets it as a particularly dark approach to summoning spirits.
In a medieval Welsh medical text marigold and cockerel bile (not blood) are mentioned in contiguous lines 54 and 55. This may well be coincidental but the recipe is worth quoting.
To knit a bone, pound pot marigold with wine and pepper and

honey and drink it for nine days. To improve the eyesight, take ground-ivy juice, and the juice of the fennel root, and greater celandine juice, and greater celandine, and sow lard and honey and a little vinegar and eel blood and cockerel bile, and put it into a vessel until it matures. That will give people their eyesight after they have lost it, the art says truly.
Luft D. *Medieval Welsh Medical Texts: Volume One: The Recipes* [Internet]. Cardiff (UK): University of Wales Press; 2020. BOOK 8, (Rac y parlis) Available from: https://www.ncbi.nlm.nih.gov/books/NBK558264/

7 This symbol belongs to the Sather Baramper Barbasan spell. Although it is square it is referred to as a 'circle'. It should be made from four parchments or calfskins.
The word AGLA at the centre was commonly used in European magic. Kate Bosse-Griffiths pointed it out as an example of the dyn hysbys' serious engagement with kabbalah, unaware of its immediate provenance. A rare Welsh example appears on a medieval silver gilt pendant found at Penhow in Gwent and now in the National Museum.
See https://museum.wales/collections/online/object/9122d9f8-5d67-3654-89b3-4b60ba4b811b/Medieval-silver-gilt-pendant/

8 A photograph of this page is reproduced on p. 44 of *Byd y Dyn Hysbys* but only the English text of the ten divine names is transcribed in the text of the book.
The Welsh text is also from the seven sisters spell and is a licence to depart for the spirits. Again, it has been interrupted by other material. Perhaps the dyn hysbys wrote the seven sisters spell on the right hand pages of his notebook and later added other material on the left hand side.

9 These slightly garbled sentences do not resemble the KJV Psalms 7 and 35. As with the Wrexham journal entry, this may illustrate the dyn hysbys' imperfect command of English.
These ten divine names are ancient and in this form go back at least to St. Jerome's 'Letter XXV. To Marcella', 'An explanation of the ten names given to God in the Hebrew Scriptures. The ten names are El, Elohim, Sabaoth, Elion, Asher yeheyeh, Adonai, Jah, the tetragram Jhvh, and Shaddai.
Divine names were used extensively in all sorts of charms and more complex rituals.

10 Bosse-Griffiths notes, 'Years went past before I was able to discover that it is referring to a book by Hieronymus Cardanus

published in Paris in 1550 and translated by William Lilly in the seventeenth century.'

11 William Lilly was taught by the Welshman John Evans. Whether the dyn hysbys knew this or not, Lilly's account of the fairy queen was included in *The Familiar Astrologer*.

The full text of Cardans' aphorisms is as follows:-

1. Life is short, Art long, Experience not easily obtained, Judgment difficult, and therefore it is necessary, that a Student not only exercise himself in considering several Figures, but also that he diligently read the writings of others who have treated rationally of this Science, and make it his business to find out the true natural causes of things by experiments, to know the certain places and processions of the Planets and Fixed Stars, Constellations, etc., but above all to be a passionate lover of truth.
2. The Principles of Art are three: Reason, Sense, and Experience, but the Principles of Operations four, viz.: The Planets, The Parts of Heaven, The Fixed Stars, and the Site or Position of all those in respect of one another.
3. There are some things perfectly known, as the Circle of Ascension; some in a competent measure, as the Revolution of the Sun; some may be known although they yet are not, as the Revolution of the Superiors; some things fall under knowledge, yet cannot be exactly known, as the precise Ingress of the Sun into the Equinoctial point; some are neither known, nor can be known, as the complete commixtures and distinct virtues of the Stars.
4. It is much worse for an Artist to conceive he knows those things which he is ignorant of, than to be ignorant of those thing which he ought to know.
5. Mean learning with an excellent judgement, avails more than a mean judgement with the greatest learning, yet is judgement with the greatest learning, yet is judgement very much assisted and perfected by learning; but everything prospers better, and is far more easily perfected that has nature for its guide and favourable stars, than that which is attempted by human industry though never so diligent.
6. He that has too great a conceit of himself will be apt to fall into many errors in his judgement; yet on the other side, he that is too diffident, is not fit for this Science.
7. He that would truly promote Art must insist as much on

the confutation of false opinions delivered by others, as in the declaration or truth.

8. An Astrologer is so far only true and honest, as he depends in his conjectures on principles of natural philosophy, and since those Arts which are inherent in their proper subjects, cannot promise any certainty concerning matters to come, the Astrologer ought never to pronounce anything absolutely or peremptorily of future contingencies.

9. Truths of themselves are to be desired, for Science itself is a certain good, now the expectation of future good very much delight us, and on the contrary, when future evils are foreseen, we may either avoid them, mitigate them, or at least bear them more contentedly.

10. Heaven is the instrument of the most High God, whereby he acts upon, and governs inferior things.

11. He that asserts things that can never be proved by experience is deceived and ambitious, but thus it always happens, those that are most ignorant of Art delights to boast of doing things different or wonderful.

12. It is all one as to promoting of Art, etc., and the knowledge thereof, either from nativities known, to predict what shall happen, or after accidents have happened, to discover the Nativities before unknown which are thereby rectified, but as to vulgar opinion, the first way far exceeds the last.

13. He that goes about to destroy Art, is far worse than he that is unskilled in it, for his mind is full of malice and idleness as well as ignorance.

14. Men may be said almost to be compelled by the Stars, even in voluntary actions, by means of their corrupt affections and ignorance.

15. Always deliver judgements from the Stars in general terms, or if thou dost otherwise let it be when thou hast very evident testimonies and in great and weighty matters.

16. We ought not to use arguments or tedious discourses in giving judgement, much less flatteries, but only to pronounce what is known by experience and firm reason.

17. A main reason why events are so rarely foretold by Astrologers, is because the Art is yet but imperfectly discovered, for hitherto those that have been most excellent in it, being commonly old persons, have despaired to live to see the fortunes of children newly-born, and the Nativities of persons grown up, being uncertain, they scarce thought them worth so much labour.

18. When true genitures exactly taken in accidents prove false or

absurd, and not agreeable to the things signified, they are to be accounted monstrous, and are to be avoided as anatomists do monstrous bodies in their dissections; for they overthrow Art.

19. Generals are to be gathered from Singulars, and Singulars from Generals, and an Artist ought always to learn to distinguish between that which is by itself, and that which is only by accident.

20. The strength and efficacy of Fixed Stars is to be considered from their magnitude, their splendours, their natures or properties, their nearness to the Ecliptic, their place in the World, their multitude, their first oriental appearance, the purity of their place, the similitude or agreement of the body or rays of a Planet with them and their circle of position.

21. The Light of the Time is the Sun in the day, and morning twilight; and the Moon in the night when she is above the Earth, and in her morning rising; so that sometimes there may be two Lights of Time, sometimes it so happens that there is none.

22. When a Planet is within five degrees of the cusp of any house, it shall be accounted to have virtue in that house though actually posited behind the cusp in another house.

23. Not only Trines and Sextiles may be counted friendly aspects, but even Squares and Oppositions too, if there happen a Reception.

The 'Choice Aphorisms' do not seem to have been widely reprinted. They may be found in G. Redway, *The Astrologer's Guide* (George Redway, 1886) p. 73-
online at https://openlibrary.org/books/OL33063040M/The_astrologer's_guide

12 Searches for Blackgrave MSS (or even Blackgrove) have drawn a blank. As a placename, Blackgrave was a hundred in the parish of East Worlington in North Devon, and also an uncommon surname.
Verses with minor differences are found in *The Familiar Astrologer* p. 611
'I subjoin the following metrical Legend of the Lunar cycles'

The Moon in Aries, life is long,
In Taurus, Gemini, Cancer, strong!
But when the Moon in Leo strives,
Full short and painful are men's lives!
In Virgo, thou'lt behold her true!
Happy and just, and amorous too!

But still men's years are short and few!
Then view her swift through Libra's speed;
The vital flame she'll constant feed,
And famous make in act and deed!
Wail! when in Scorpio she pursues,
The Sagittarian arrow! Thews,
And sinews potent grace this latter sign!
Long life and happy then is thine!
In Capricornius, in Aquarius short,
But Pisces constant wards the fatal dart!

Either the dyn hysbys or, more likely, Kate Bosse-Griffiths, has mistranscribed 'Mercary'. *The Familiar Astrologer* has 'Merurii'. The Mercurii were a small esoteric group in the early nineteenth century centred around Robert Cross Smith and others. The charm itself was not included by Kate Bosse-Griffiths but it is undoubtedly 'A Charm Sung By Witches' that I have included below. This is one of a few spells that appear in *The Familiar Astrologer* by Raphael p.215

This charm occurs on the page after the Bartholomew charm against thieves included in Llyfr Cyfrin p. 123-125.

A CHARM SUNG BY WITCHES WHILE GATHERING HERBS FOR MAGICAL PURPOSES.

Hail to thee, holy herb,
Growing on the ground,
All on Mount Calvary
First wast thou found.
Thou art good for many sores,
And healeth many a wound;
In the name of St. Jesu!
I take thee from the ground.

The muttering of this charm, while concocting drugs or simples, balsams or elixirs, contributes marvellously to their efficacy. A version specific to picking vervain was printed in John White, *The Way to The True Church*, 1608.

Hallowed be thou, Vervein, as thou growest on the ground,
For in the mount of Calvary there was thou first found.
Thou healedst our Saviour Jesus Christ, and stanchedst his

THE
FAMILIAR ASTROLOGER;

AN EASY GUIDE

TO

FATE DESTINY, & FOREKNOWLEDGE,

AS WELL AS TO THE

SECRET AND WONDERFUL PROPERTIES OF NATURE.

Embellished with curious Engravings on Steel, and numerous Wood Cuts.

By RAPHAEL.

Author of that celebrated Book, "The Astrologer of the Nineteenth Century," "The Popular Manual of Astrology," "The Prophetic Messenger," &c. &c. Member of the Astronomical Society of London, of the Philosophical Lyceum, of the "Mercurii," and of several other learned Associations.

London:
PRINTED FOR JOHN BENNETT,
THREE-TUN PASSAGE, IVY LANE, PATERNOSTER ROW,
AND SOLD BY ALL BOOKSELLERS.

1832.

bleeding wound;
In the name of the Father, the Son, and the holy Ghost, I take thee from the ground.

13 *The Familiar Astrologer* was itself an anthology of issues of *The Astrologer*, published by Raphael. The selections in Llyfr Cyfrin are all from volume IV of *The Astrologer*, published in 1831. That volume also includes astrology, geomancy, occult-related historical anecdotes and short stories. The same issue includes William Lilly's account of an invocation of the fairy queen and, in a selection of tales about fairies, one titles 'Y Tylwyth Teg' which is taken, perhaps indirectly, from Edward Davies *The Mythology and Rites of the British Druids*, 1809.

This spell and a handful of other selections were included by Frederick Hockley in his manuscript *Occult Spells*, also without credit. *Occult Spells* was begun in 1829.
Kate Bosse-Griffiths summarised parts of the spell (as may be seen in the text I included, so here is the spell as it appears in *The Familiar Astrologer*.

A MAGICAL EXPERIMENT.
The following strange experiment is copied from a very scarce and curious manuscript. In the present enlightened age, the rehearsal thereof cannot possibly do any harm, as we presume it would be difficult to find any one who would go through the disgusting process of " raising the dead spirit," even should they place faith in its performance. It is word for word with the original, which was deemed a most profound secret, in the reign of Popery and Inquisition; the betrayal of which would have subjected the party to imprisonment for life, or to a cruel death.

TO INVOCATE AND CONVERSE WITH THE DEAD.
"When any one dieth, whom you would have the spirit of when dead, Go wheare the grave will be made, and make sure to take a handful of the first earth tbat is digged when the grave is first begun to be made; then rehearsing the person's name that is dead, saying as followeth:—
" 'O (N) I doe take of the earth in which thou must enter into, tbat thy spirit may come unto the churche to speake unto me, and fulfill my will, and that it shall never have power to rest, or be quiet until thou come to speak with me, and fulfill my will and commandments.'
"Afterwards goe into the churche with the earthe in thy hande,

and there beholde untill the bodie of the dead person be brought into the Churche; and thou shall see a two-foulde spirit cominge. And the Spirit of the dead like Catts. Then rehearse the names of God followinge, afterwardes they will departe and go with the funerall to the grave. But thou must beholde still, and walke untill the corpse be buried, and every one departed, and gone awaye.

"Then the Spirit will come to thee again, whom doe not feare, for it cannot hurte thee. Then calle it by the person's name that is buried, and say as followeth,

" 'O (N) I doe conjure thee by the Passion of our Lord Jesus Xt, and by the virginitie of the sweet Virgin Marye, and by the twelve Apostles, and by the four Evangelists, and by all Martyrs and Confessors, and by this Earthe which I have in my hande, which is of the Earthe wherein thy bodie is buried in, O (N) and by all the Constellations of heaven, and by all the Virtues and Powers, which are in heaven and earth, and by all the Angelles, and their falle, in which was the cause of Man's creation, and by the wordes which Christ spake as he hung on the Altar of the Crosse, That is, Ely, Ely, Lama-zabacthani, Semiforas, that thou doe not offende me by any manner of lyinge or deceit, but that thou declare the truth of all things that I shall aske thee, and that thou doe come unto me at all times when I doe calle thee, by this name, O (N). And in answeringe me trulye with an understanding voice, and true tongue or speeche, which I do best understande, and thus I doe bind thee and conjure thee by all the wordes aforesaid, and I commande thee by our Lord Jesus Xt, and by his most precious bloude, and by him that will come to judge the quicke and the deade, and the worlde by fier. Amen."

" Then carrye the earth in thy hande to the grave again, and say unto him, Go in peace, O (N), and the peace of God be between me and thee, and as often as I will speake with thee, be thou readie, and when I call thee by this name O (N) with this conjuration, Go in peace, and the crosse of Xt. be betweene me and thee, nowe and always. Amen. Fiat, fiat, fiat."

" Note firste of all when the spirits do appeare, rehearse these names of God followinge to bind them, and thou shalt be safe from all dangers afterwardes. These be the names followinge. 1

" Tetragrammaton, Anronadall, Draconium, Alliam, fortissam, fortisson, figa, Sache, frege, Pronis-sioni, Sucreon, Dracosu, Eloy, Sachee, Emanuell, Anathanathout, Semaforas. Amen."

14 'Another strange Necromantic Spell' follows on directly from the previous spell in *The Familiar Astrologer*. The text is as

follows:

ANOTHER STRANGE NECROMANTIC SPELL.
"If thou be disposed to speake or meete with anye person lyvinge or deade, you muste goe into the Churche yarde on a frydaye at night, at 9 or 10 of the Clocke, and walke rounde aboute the alley seven times, and when you come to a corner, you muste stande still, and saye the Lordes prayer, and the Creede, and before you have gone seven times aboute, you shall meete them you woulde meete withpierall, personallye as they were wont to goe. Finis."
The Familiar Astrologer p. 217

15 'Another strange Necromantic Spell' follows on directly from the previous spell in *The Familiar Astrologer*. It is included in the text above.

16 Again, this comes from the same section of *The Familiar Astrologer*. As it has not been copied exactly by the dyn hysbys, here is *the Familiar Astrologer* version. This was also included in Sarah Hewitt, *Nummits And Crummits: Devonshire Customs, Characteristics, and Folk-Lore*, (T. Burleigh 1900)

The sufferings of Jacob to-day be my speed.
The devotion of the holy Lamb thieves shall let,
The strength of Jesus's passion them beset,
The dread of death hold thieves low,
The wisdom of Solomon cause their overthrow.
The sufferings of Job set them in hold,
The chastity of Daniel let what they would.
The speech of Isaac their speech shall spill,
The languishing faith of Jerome let them of their will.
The flaming fires of hell to hit them, I bequeath,
The deepness of the deep sea, their hearts to grieve
The help of Heaven cause thieves to stand.
He that made the sun and moon bind them with his hand
So sure as St. Bartholomew bound the fiend,
With the hair of his beard.
With these three sacred names of God known and unknown.
Miser, Suell, Tetragrammaton, Christ Jesus ! Amen.
From a Curious Manuscript
The Familiar Astrologer p.218

17 Thus Words being spoke with great reverence 57
These might be the words of the author as they are close to the

Wrexham journal entry and he has similar problems with the perfect tense and spelling.

18 I refer to this journal entry several times in the book. (See page 164 onwards and page 180 onwards.) Shon y Rhoses was a historical person. 'Dids' are teats or udders. Bosse-Griffiths comments that she has changed the spelling a little.

19 Aside from more formal magical rituals of compulsion like this, there were widespread folk practices for divining the identity of one's future partner known as 'rhamanta', 'romancing'.
Kate Bosse-Griffiths comments, 'This is a personal charm, and it can be practised by a man or woman alone and in his own room, and the only visible means required are the paper and new pins and the blood and the fire. The invisible means are the wish, the will, the perseverance, the number seven – and the spirits...
The names of the ghosts seem rather intimidating, but the exact same names can be seen in Francis Barrett's book, *The Magus*, published in 1801, and I saw that this book was be one of those possessed by the Dyn Hysbys of Denbighshire.
The names actually come from the *Heptameron*, which was Francis Barrett's source for including them in *The Magus*. The *Heptameron* was translated into Welsh as part of the *Fourth Book of Occult Philosophy* compendium and published in 1830 in Robert Roberts' *Seryddiaeth*. Curiously, the version in *Seryddiaeth* lacks the names of the ministers below Sarabotes, so it cannot be the immediate source for our dyn hysbys. Spirit names and components from more complicated grimoire rituals were often repurposed for folk magic usage and that seems to be what has happened here.

20 The figure is ultimately from the *Discoverie of Witchcraft*
This was commonly used in the written charms used for unwitching and preventing witchcraft on cattle. Kate Bosse-Griffiths offers no context for the charm but as it was likely to already be known to the dyn hysbys perhaps it was intended to protect the notebook from malign influences (this is pure speculation on my part.) See the chapter on cattle healing for more on this.

Tylwyth Teg and Dynion Hysbys

The Tylwyth Teg, the fair tribe or family, often rendered in English as the fair folk, were tricksters who existed outside of the spiritual hierarchy of Christianity.[1] They were not merely the subjects of entertaining folktales but were believed by many people to exist. For most people encounters with the fairies were to be avoided. Stories of the fairies[2] usually function as cautionary tales. For ordinary people no good comes of encounters with the fairies.[3] The one category of people in Wales who were able to liaise with fairies, who could influence or at least knew their ways and understood the rules and restrictions that governed them, and hence knew how to exploit the loopholes in the laws of the Tylwyth Teg, was that of the magician.

A typical Welsh fairy story follows the pattern: something goes wrong; a dyn hysbys is called in to help; the dyn hysbys recognises the hand of the Tylwyth Teg and instructs the victim or the victim's family or friends to perform some act that lies outside the bounds of ordinary life; the wrong is undone (though there may be a twist).

There were various attempts to explain the existence of the Tylwyth Teg, to rationalise them or to relate them to existing religious concepts. Thus the Tylwyth might be seen as spirits, even if they had corporeal qualities[4], or as the dead (dead relatives were sometimes seen in the fairy otherworld) or as devils, or as fallen angels, or were in later times euhemerised as the memories of a pygmy tribe or as the spirits of long-passed druids.[5]

The Tylwyth Teg could be encountered in isolated places or in unexpected circumstances. They might offer access to a realm, an otherworld, that was underground or beneath a lake or within a cave. It might be filled with marvels. They could offer gifts and treasures but they were dangerous to deal with. Friendships and acquisitions granted in the fairy realm were rarely transferable to the everyday world. There were prohibitions associated with the fairies. They didn't like iron. Their women didn't like to be struck (and who can blame them?) They took human babies and left sour, ugly, awkward changelings in return.

Wales has some of the oldest tales that involve figures recognisable as fairies. Before the adoption of the term Tylwyth Teg, fairy-style traditions are found in Wales in the works of Gerald of Wales (1146-1223) and Walter Map (1140-c.1209). Gerald of Wales' Elidyr (the Welsh equivalent of the name Elidorus in Gerald's Latin) who spoke a language similar to Greek, or Walter Map's Gwestin Gwestiniog (Brychan Brycheiniog) and his otherworldly wife clearly belong to the fairy tradition but aren't referred to as Tylwyth Teg or as fairies or as any Latin equivalent and there are also several other terms used for fairy-like entities.

The tale of Elidyr exemplifies the otherworld journey, while that of Gwestin is our earliest version of what has come to be known as the Fairy Bride legend. Gerald tells us that the boy of his tale was Elidyr a priest and that it happened shortly before Gerald's time. Gerald seems to have got the story from David II, Bishop of St David's, who said that whenever Elidyr told him the story he burst into tears as he remembered the language of the 'little folk'.

When he was 12 years old and a trainee priest Elidyr hid in a hollow river bank for two days to escape the beating his teacher would have given him for being such a bad pupil. Two small men appeared to him and told him that if he followed them they would take him to a country of delights and sports. A path led through darkness to a beautiful land that was full of rivers and meadows and woods and plains but was gloomy in the daytime and completely dark in the night due to the lack of the sun and moon and stars. Elidyr was brought to the king who, after assessing him, had him play with his own son. All the people were small but well-proportioned, fair in complexion with shoulder length hair. Their horses and greyhounds were also beautiful but small. They lived on milk and saffron and spoke a language that resembled Greek.

Elidyr often returned home to his mother in our world, at first accompanied by people from that land, later on his own. One day she asked him to bring some gold from the other realm. Elidorus stole the golden ball with which he and the king's son used to play. He ran back to his home but as he crossed the threshold, he tripped and dropped the ball whereupon it was seized by two of the small people who had been chasing him. Never again was he able to find the path to the other kingdom.[6]

Gwestin Gwestiniog is to be identified with king Brychan Brycheiniog, whose name gives us the kingdom of Brycheiniog, still the Welsh for the county known in English as Brecknockshire. Gwestin saw women dancing for three nights in a row on the shore of Llyn Safaddon (in English Lake Llangorse or Brecknock Mere) before they disappeared into the lake. He learned the secret of catching them and on the third night held on to one of them and took her as his wife. They had children together but when he struck her with a bridle piece, as she had predicted, she left him and returned to the lake with their children. He was able to keep hold of their son Triunein, who remained with his father and later attended the king of Deheubarth. Triunein disappeared during a battle and was believed not to have died but to have returned to the lake.[7]

The very most famous of Welsh fairy stories is that of Llyn y Fan Fach, recorded considerably later than the two preceding medieval tales, in the nineteenth century. A fairy bride marries a Welsh farmer and brings her superb cattle with her. There are conditions on the way in which she must be wooed (with bread that is half-baked) and if he strikes her three times, as he does in non-intuitive ways, she must return below the waters of the lake. As with the story of Gwestin, the unnamed woman returns to her home beneath the lake but the children remain behind. Their fairy mother returns from time to time and teaches them the lore of healing. The physicians of the Myddfai, a dynasty of healers and doctors who arguably continued into the nineteenth century, claimed descent from the woman of the lake.

The tales are not wholly separate from the greater body of Welsh lore, of myth and legend. There are other versions of the fairy bride legend in Wales, anchored to various locales. The Llyn Safaddon story is one of many tales linked to Brychan Brycheiniog and his children. Journeys to the otherworld and marriage between earthly men and otherworldly brides, with its attendant clash of cultures, are staples of Welsh mythology.

If we look at the First Branch of the Mabinogi, we have (possibly) earlier or contemporaneous tales with elements of both of these story types. Pwyll makes a journey to the otherworld of Annwn after he meets its king Arawn at Gorsedd Arberth. Later in the story he encounters a woman on a horse with whom he cannot catch up. She is Rhiannon, who is clearly otherworldly (although it is not said that she comes from Annwfn) and who eventually marries Pwyll, not without the intervention of some otherworldly obstructions. Rhiannon is mistreated after their newborn child is stolen away. In the Third Branch Rhiannon and her son Pryderi are imprisoned in an otherworld. Although the outcomes may be different, the challenges are similar.

The Tylwyth Teg are referred to several times in Llyfr Cyfrin. I have left these references as they are rather than render them as 'fairies' to allow the reader to retain a more specifically Welsh version of the fairies.

The association of the Tylwyth Teg with the dyn hybsys or consiriwr, the cunning man or conjuror is a classic trope of Welsh fairydom. Fairy-like creatures have long had magical associations. Anglo-Saxon elves were appealed to in early charms against fever. In Scotland fairies were magical familiars and sources of magical knowledge. In early modern England magicians treated fairies as spirits who, like other types of spirits, could help them find buried treasure. This also occurred in Wales, as can be seen by the spell in Llyfr Cyfrin 'Another way of calling upon the spirits called the Tylwyth Teg and to discover hidden treasure', which calls upon seven fairy sisters.

A fifteenth century poem 'Y Niwl Hudolus' ('The Magical Mist') was inspired by the great medieval poet Dafydd ap Gwilym's 'Y Niwl' ('The Mist'). It is written in an imitation of his style and so qualifies as part of the Dafydd ap Gwilym apocrypha. This first recorded usage of Tylwyth Teg also happens to be the earliest association between magicians and fairies in Wales. The mist in 'Y Niwl Hudolus' is compared to a magician,

> Fal hudol byd yn hedeg
> O barthlwyth y Tylwyth Teg,[8]
> Like a magician of a world flying from the dwelling of the Tylwyth Teg.[9]

This association of Welsh magicians with the Tylwyth Teg spanned centuries and attributed a level of control and influence by the magician. There seems to have been little interest in fairy magic in England or Scotland after the early modern period. The evidence shows that, not only was there a dyn hysbys active in the 1830s who was very interested in fairy magic (the one who wrote the Llyfr Cyfrin), there was an extensive folklore tradition concerning the interaction of magicians and fairies.[10]

These two types of sources–historical evidence and the folklore tradition–will be described separately.

HISTORICAL CASES

It was only while working on a final draft of this chapter that I realised how extraordinary it is that we have any historical records at all of Welsh fairy magic–after all, it seems like this is a phenomenon that might have bypassed historical records entirely. The nature of our sources gives us more evidence concerning deceptive or criminal examples of alleged fairy magic. Clients who were satisfied with the way in which a dyn hysbys had intervened with the Tylwyth Teg were unlikely to take them to court.

Two examples involve fraudulent appeal to the fairies. These, and folklore accounts are our main sources of surviving material on the relationship between magicians and the Tylwyth Teg.

Ann Jones was indicted for felonious witchcraft and for fraud in 1635 at the Denbighshire Great Sessions court. It transpired that she would take money from her victims, promising to return it and would then move on to another locale. It was under the name of Ann Jones that she was charged, but in court she denied that her name was Ann Jones but said her real name was Elen Gilbert. Her motive for defrauding her clients was that she needed money as her husband had been away for a long time and she had had children by several different men.

Gruffyth ap Owen of Corwen had a child who was sick and lame in both legs. Ann told him that if he would lend her some money she would show it to the fairies, who would heal the child, and would then return the coins, which amounted to 40 shillings in gold and five shillings nine pence in silver. She did not give back the money and when Gruffyth tracked her down she only had 20 shillings left.

John Lewys of Bryneglwys had a similar story. Ann told his wife that their daughter had a disease that would be dangerous if it were not prevented. Ann was given nine shillings and a piece of woolen cloth worth ten shillings. The child breathed on the coins and they would be shown to the fairies, who would free the girl from her sickness, and then they would be returned. But she never did give back the money. The child's breath on the coins would have provided the convincing detail of a magical link between the child and the fairies. Ann was probably poor and in need, but so were her cheated clients.

By the next year 1636 Harry Lloyd was in trouble for the same kind of offence. Harry's claims were grander and more detailed than those of Ann Jones. Harry described himself as a scholar but others thought him a common wanderer. He was known as a surgeon and diviner and specialised in finding lost objects and divination. He made his reputation when he restored a rough linen sheet to a woman who had lost it, returning it to her back door early one morning. Harry also consorted with spirits and familiars and the Tylwyth Teg. Harry conned one client out of two shillings by telling him he needed the money for wax for candles (to be purchased in Pwllheli) that were necessary for the ritual in which he would summoned the spirits, which he did at night. The candles and the mention of a circle recall classic spirit conjuring techniques.

The colourful and dramatic language of the court account makes it worth quoting.

> He the said Harry lloyd being a common wanderer and vagabond from place to place having no certain trade occupation or means of living but under feigned colour and pretence of surgery or Physic doth exercise wicked

& unlawful arts (that is to say) fortunetelling, Palmistry, common haunting and familiarity with wicked spirits in the night time and common cheatings and cozenages of diverse of his majesties leadgeliege? people...whereby he is dangerous to the inferior sorte of people ...

this examiniate demanded of the said Harry Lloyd how & by what means he made them so rich. he informed that by familiars and spirits and certain fairies commonly called in welsh (y Tyllwyth Teg) and that he the said Harry Lloyd did resort unto them & had conferences with them Twice every week in the night time viz upon Tuesday nights and the Thursday nights weekly through the year and that the fairies and spirits put a great quantity of gold & Silver upon the anvil of said Richard y gof? every night thorough the year, where the said Richard found them every morning accordingly. And also that the said fairies and spirits did always every night put into a hole in the hedge of the church yard of Llanvaglan much gold and silver, where the said Richard ap Evan found it every morning likewise. And the said Harry Lloyd used, as he said, to visit the said Richard y Gove and Evan ap richard twice or thrice every year, asking that each of them will give the said Harry Lloyd sometimes ten shillings sometimes five shillings at every time. . . ..

The notable astrologer William Lilly was taught his art by a Welshman, John Evans (not to be confused with 'Arise' Evans who lived at the same time, was known for his prophecies and criticised Lilly in print.) Evans was an extraordinary character, described by Lilly as 'the most saturnine person my eyes ever beheld, either before I practised or since; of a middle stature; broad forehead, beetle-browed, thick shoulders, flat nosed, full lips, down-looked, black curling stiff hair, splay-footed; to give him his right, he had the most piercing judgment naturally upon a figure of theft, and many other questions, that I ever met withal; yet for money he would willingly give contrary judgments, was much addicted to debauchery, and then very abusive and quarrelsome, seldom without a black eye, or one mischief of other...'[11]

Lilly, while relating the scrying of Sarah Skelhorn, mentions that Ellen Evans, the daughter of John Evans, had previously scryed for him. 'Ellen Evans, daughter of my tutor Evans, her call unto the crystal was this:

> O Micol, O tu Micol, regina pigmeorum veni, &c.
> O Micol, O thou Micol, Queen of the Pygmies, come.

Lilly does not specify her age at this time but it is possible that she was still a girl, as it was common practice to use virgin children as scryers. Ellen Evans, and presumably her father John Evans, was appealing to the Queen of the Fairies, Micol, who appears three centuries later in the Llyfr Cyfrin as Micob. Lilly goes on to give an account of an invocation of the Queen of the Fairies. It is not clear from Lilly's account whether Ellen Evans was a girl or a woman at the time. If she was a girl she would fit the model of the child-scryer, well known in magical texts from the Greek Magical Papyri into the medieval and Renaissance grimoires. Nor does Lilly relate whether Ellen Evans performed the invocation alone or if she was at the service of John Evans. It was usual practice for a scryer to work with a magician so it is quite possible that Ellen was doing the scrying for her father. John Evans operated around roughly the same time as Harry Lloyd. This was a fertile period for genuine and fraudulent interactions between magicians and fairies in Wales and England.[12]

Some later accounts of charmers and conjurors show that their dealings with the Tylwyth Teg were seen as somewhat disreputable but were not as serious as consorting with demons. As Dan Harms has commented, rituals that summoned demons and other dangerous spirits were long and complex.

Nevertheless, shorter conjurations with fewer ritual

trappings are common, and many–though certainly not all–of the operations connected to fairies fall into this category.

This is notable for two reasons. First, it suggests that the magicians perceived fairies to be easier to summon, perhaps due to their nature as creatures associated with this world, rather than with heaven or hell. Second, the same magicians were not particularly concerned that a conjuration of a fairy would inadvertently produce an infernal spirit.'[13]

The Independent Calvinist minister Edmund Jones recorded many examples of apparitions and supernatural encounters in eighteenth century Monmouthshire. Charles Hugh of Llangybi and Rhisiart Cap Du (Richard Black Cap) of Aberystruth were notable local magical practitioners in the locale.

> Rhisiart went out to meet the fairies through a hole in his thatched roof, so it was said, although he claimed only to observe the stars through the hole. On one occasion ('as was the custom then in those days of ignorance') Rhisiart Cap Du was fetched to charm a person greatly hurt after inadvertently falling among the fairies. When Rhisiart Cap Du entered the house, the sick man flung a weight at the charmer with all his might, saying 'Thou old villain was one of the worst of them to hurt me.'[14]

Charles Hugh was credited with supernatural knowledge of when the fairies were abroad.

> Henry Edmund, of Hafodafel, was one night visiting Charles Hugh, the conjuror of Aberystruth, and they walked together as far as Lanhiddel, where Hugh tried to persuade his companion to stay all night with him at a public house. Edmund refused, and said he would go home. 'You had better stay,' said Hugh in a meaning tone. But Edmund went out into the street, when he was seized by invisible hands and borne through the air to Landovery, in Carmarthenshire, a distance of fully fifty

miles as the crow flies. There he was set down at a public house where he had before been, and talked with people who knew him. He then went out into the street, when he was seized again and borne back to Lanhiddel, arriving there the next morning at day-break. The first man he met was the conjuror Charles Hugh, who said, 'Did I not tell you you had better stay with me?'[15]

Fairy encounters were dangerous for most but could be a source of knowledge for conjurors.

They appeared diverse ways, but their most frequent way of appearing was like dancing Companies with Musick, and in the form of Funerals. When they appeared like dancing Companies, they were desirous to entice persons into their Company, and some were drawn among them and remained among them some time; usually a whole year; as did Edmund William Rees, a Man whom I well knew, and was a Neighbour, who came back at the year's end, and looked very bad. But either they were not able to give much account of themselves or they durst not give it, only said they had been dancing, and that the time was short. But there were some others who went with them at night and returned some times at night, and sometimes the next morning; especially those persons who took upon them to cure the hurts received from the Fairies, as Charles Hugh of Coed yr Pame in Langybi Parish. And Rissiart Cap Dee [Du] of Aberystruth, for the former of these must certainly converse with them, For how else could he declare the words which his visiters had spoken a day or days before they came to him, to their great surprize and wonder?[16]

Fairies had not been understood to be as abhorrent as demons or other spirits but the Protestant revivals that spread across Wales in the eighteenth and nineteenth centuries were increasingly suspicious of the Tylwyth Teg. On the one hand they were seen as a remnant of Catholic belief that persisted when the cult of saints or Catholic folk magic or other 'superstitions' had considerably diminished. On the other hand, the new chapel culture was hostile to the older cheerful, boozy forms of Welsh culture. Dancing to the harp would be seen as worldy and licentious, to be replaced by hymn singing. Many people had encountered fairies dancing in the wilderness. Fairies were often perceived as being dressed in clothes that were out of fashion or belonged to older generations. In the same way, they continued to dance to the harp just as the older generations had in Merry Wales.

W.Y. Evans-Wentz, in his 1911 *The Fairy Faith in Celtic Countries*, offers an example of a dyn hysbys using the Tylwyth Teg for divination. His reports are generalised, lacking much in the way of specific detail, but he does credit the following to T. M. Morgan's *The History and Antiquities of the Parish of Newchurch* (Carmarthen, 1910)

John Harries of Cwrt-y-cadno in Carmarthenshire was the most renowned dyn hysbys of the nineteenth century. His book containing containing the spirit lists and seals of the seventeenth century grimoires Goetia and Theurgia-Goetia is in the National Library at Aberystwyth, while there is an extensive body of folklore concerning him. This is the only instance that I know of in which John Harries Cwrt-y-cadno is credited with relations with the fairies rather than with 'spirits', usually in a general way.

> Tylwyth Teg Divination.–The second narrative I quote:–'A farmer of this neighbourhood having lost his cattle, went to consult y dyn hysbys (a diviner), in Cardiganshire, who was friendly with the fairies. Whenever the fairies visited the diviner they foretold future events, secrets, and the whereabouts of lost property. After the farmer reached the diviner's house the diviner showed him the fairies, and then when the diviner had consulted them he told the farmer to go home as soon as he could and that he would find the cattle in such and such a

place. The farmer did as he was directed, and found the cattle in the very place where the dyn hysbys told him they would be.' And the third narrative asserts that a man in the parish of Trelech who was fraudulently excluded by means of a false will from inheriting the estate of his deceased father, discovered the defrauder and recovered the estate, solely through having followed the advice given by the Tylwyth Teg, when (again as in the above account) they were called up as spirits by a dyn hysbys, a Mr. Harries, of Cwrt y Cadno, a place near Aberystwyth.[17]

This single association of John Harries with the fairies recently had a surprising revival in mainstream Welsh culture in 2022. Described as 'an accessible adventure for families taking place at Bryngarw Country Park this Halloween.... Part treasure hunt, part theatre production...' *The Conjuror of Cwrtycadno/Dyn Hysbys Cwrtycadno* draws directly on the above tradition.

Whilst researching her ancestry in the National Library of Wales a young woman named Heledd Harries discovered a book by her Great Great Great Great Grandfather. A book of incantations! Heledd knew nothing of the magic in her blood or the trouble she was about to cause. Now we need your help to get hundreds of bewildered Tylwyth Teg home before Nos Calan Gaeaf.[18]

Bi-lingual and with British Sign Language, this inclusive event must have been a lot of fun for kids around Bridgend. It seems that in twenty-first-century Wales interaction with the Tylwyth Teg is no longer the preserve of the dyn hysbys but is now practised occasionally by children!

The many instances of magicians dealing with the Tylwyth Teg in folktale will be dealt with in the next chapter.[19]

Notes

1 C.S. Lewis, *The Discarded Image* p. 122.
'On fairies, for whom he uses the Latin name the Longaevi, the long-lived, They are marginal, fugitive creatures. They are perhaps the ony creatures to whom the Model — the grand, inclusive cosmology of medieval Christianity — does not assign, as it were, an official status. Herein lies their imaginative value. They soften the classic severity of the huge design. They intrude a welcome hint of wildness into a universe that is in danger of being a little too self-explanatory, too luminous.'
This marginal nature of fairies allowed them to exist within an otherwise Christian world, although protestantism was later particularly hostile to fairies. Despite the attempts listed above to rationalise the place of fairies in the world, they never quite fit in. Daniel Harms comments, 'As with so many other spiritual entities, the queens of the fairies were approached in Europe through the ritual practice pursued outside officially sanctioned religion. Many such practices were likely orally transmitted and lost before they could be recorded.
Sorita d'Este and David Rankine (eds.) *The Faerie Queens : A Collection of Essays Exploring the Myths, Magic and Mythology of The Faerie Queens* (Avalonia, 2013) p. 55.
2 'Fairy tales' has acquired such a very broad meaning that many of the most famous fairy tales such as Hansel and Gretel, Jack and the Beanstalk and Little Red Riding Hood do not involve fairies.
3 As Ireland's most renowned contemporary expert in fairies, Eddie Lenihan, replied when asked if he had ever seen fairies, 'No. And I hope I never do.'
4 In the medieval world spirits themselves could have corporeal qualities. Gerald of Wales ponders how a soothsayer from Caerleon named Meilyr 'was able to see these demons with the eyes of his head. Spirits cannot be seen with our physical eyes, unless they themselves assume corporeal substance.' Gerald of Wales, Lewis Thorpe (trans.) *The Journey Through Wales/The Description of Wales* (Penguin, 1978) p. 120.
5 'Our Pembrokeshire witness is a maiden Welshwoman, sixty years old, who speaks no English, but a university graduate, her nephew, will act as our interpreter. ... 'Spirits and fairies exist all round us invisible .... I think the spirits around us are the fallen

ngels, for when Doctor Harris [sic] died his books on witchcraft had to be burned in order to free the place where he lived from evil spirits. The fairies, too, are sometimes called fallen angels. They will do good to those who befriend them, and harm others. I think there must be an intermediate state between life on earth and heavenly life, and it may be in this that spirits and fairies live.'
W.E. Evans-Wentz, *The Fairy Faith in Celtic Countries* (The Lost Library, 2010) pp. 153-154, online at https://www.gutenberg.org/files/34853/34853-h/34853-h.htm)
 The story is part of the modern repetoire of Welsh fairy story chiefly due to its inclusion in W. Jenkyn Thomas' *The Welsh Fairy Book* (A. & C. Black, 1938).
 In Walter Map's text the name is given as Wastin Wastiniac, which in modern welsh would be Gwestin Gwestiniog.
 Helen Fulton, *Selections From the Dafydd ap Gwilym Apocrypha* (Gomer Press, 1996), pp. 120-121, ll. 27-40).
 The entities in folk belief and literature that are referred to as Fairies in English are principally known in Wales as y Tylwyth Teg. The Welsh 'tylwyth' is defined by *Geiriadur Prifysgol Cymru* as '(extended) family, kinsfolk, tribe, lineage; household, retinue, followers; also fig.' A native Welsh speaker from Carmarthenshire told me that she refers to her family as 'tylwyth' rather than the more usual 'teulu'.
Tylwyth derives etymologically from tŷ 'house' + llwyth; the latter word has a similar semantic range to tylwyth, 'tribe, lineage, family, clan, (hereditary) caste, people, nation, inhabitants.' Thus, 'house clan' might not be a bad literal translation.
Teg means 'fair, beautiful, pretty, handsome, fine, neat; agreeable, amiable, dear, pleasant; fine (of the weather), dry, hot; clean, pure; flattering (of words, &c.), plausible. '
It is possible that 'Teg', which often translates the English 'fair' as in fair of appearance, was a misunderstanding of the English 'fairy', which has complex etymology, ultimately deriving from the French, and did not originally refer to their fair appearances. Thus Tylwyth Teg might be essentially a borrowing from English. This was argued by W.J. Gruffydd and reiterated by Richard Suggett in his essay 'The Fair Folk and Enchanters' in Young, Simon and Houlbrook, Ceri (ed.) *Magical Folk: British and Irish Fairies* (Gibson Square, 2018) p. 138.
The term first appears in 'Y Niwl Hudolus', 'The Magical Mist', a poem which was formerly ascribed to the great Dafydd ap Gwilym but is now assigned as part of his apocrypha, i.e. poems that resemble those of Dafydd ap Gwilym, deliberately imitating them, but aren't written by him. However, the appearance of the small people who Elidorus met was described as fair (at least in the English translation of Gerald's Latin.)
In Y Niwl Dafydd refers to them as 'Tylwyth Gwyn' and as 'ellyllon'. This is usually taken to mean the 'tylwyth' of Gwyn (ap Nudd). Gwyn ap

Nudd was later seen as king of the fairies. However, it could be the descriptive adjective white, in which case it is a very short leap from describing them as gwyn 'white' to 'teg' fair. Dafydd refers in 'Y Niwl' to Tylwyth Gwyn, 'the tribe of Gwyn', which may also be read as 'the white tribe'. It may have been a short leap to paraphrase this as 'tylwth teg', 'fair tribe', for the sake of the internal rhyme and alliteration that occurs in the Welsh poetic techniques that comprise cynghanedd. 'O barthlwyth y Tylwyth Teg,' is cynghanedd sain in which the line is divided into three parts, the first section rhyming with the second and the consonants of the third section of the line echoing those of the second. Other names for them include dynon bach teg, ellyllon, bendith y mamau/bendith eu mamau, Plant Rhŷs Dwfn and others. Y Teulu and Tylwyth Gwyn, the family and the white tribe, are others.

10 We may note, however, that in the only journal entry in the Llyfr Cyfrin excerpts the farmer from hope near Wrexham complains that 'his cattle and milk had been witched', not that the fairies were causing trouble.

11 The original text:

He the said harry lloyd beinge a common wanderer & vagabond from place to place having noe c'teine trade occupacon or meanes of livinge but under fayned colour & p'tence of surgery or Phisike doth exercise wicked & unlawfull arts (that is to say) fortunetellinge, Palmestry common hauntinge & familiarity wth wicked spirits in the night time & common cheatings & cusnages of div'se of his mats leadge people…whereby he is dangerous to the inferiour sorte of people … this exaiate demannded of the said harry lloyd how & by what meanes he made them soe rich. he informed that by familiars and spirits and c'teine fairies commonly called in welsh (y Tyllwith Tegg) & that he the said harry Lloyd did resort unto them & had conferrences wth them Twice everie weeke in the night time vidzt upon Tuesday nights & the Thursday nights weekelie thorough the yeere and that the fayries & spirits put a great quantitiy of gould & Silv' uppon the anville of said Richard y goe everie night thorough the yeere, where the said Richard found them everie morning accordingly. And alsoe that the said fayries and spirits did always everie night putt into a hole in the hedge of the church yeard of Llanvaglan much gould and silver, where the said Richard ap Evan found it everie morninge likewise. And the said Harry Lloyd useth, as he said, to visit the said Richard y Gove and Evan ap richard twice or thrice everie yeere, asking that each of them will give the said

Harry Lloyd sometimes tenn shillings sometimes five shillings att everie time. . . .
Richard Suggett, *Welsh Witches:: Narratives of Witchcraft and Magic from sixteenth- and seventeenth-century Wales* (Atramentous Press, 2018) p187
12 Lilly, William (Katherine Briggs, ed.) The Last of the Astrologer (The Folklore Society, 1974) p.320 Gutenburg edition https://www.gutenberg.org/files/15835/15835-h/15835-h.htm
For an extensive account of fraudulent association with fairies in seventeenth century England, see J. Kent Clark's *Goodwin Wharton (Penguin, 1989)*. Clark gives an extensive and dryly humorous straight account of Mary Parish's relations with Wharton. She truly led him up the garden path in an endless quest for fairy treasure. Wharton's unpublished autobiography runs to 500,000 words and spanned 18 years.
13 Dan Harms, 'Hell and Fairy' in *Knowing Demons Kmowing Spirits* (Palgrave MacMillan 2018) p.77
14 The Appearance of Evil p. 86; A Geographical, Historical, and Religious Account of the Parish of Aberystruth p. 70-71 PDF
15 History of Aberystruth p. 70.
16 Ibid.
17 W.Y. Evans-Wentz, *The Fairy-Faith in Celtic Countries*, p. 150-151
https://www.sacred-texts.com/neu/celt/ffcc/ffcc124.htm
Suggett, 'The Fair Folk and Enchanters' in *Magical Folk* p. 144
18 https://www.takingflighttheatre.org.uk/cwrtycadno/ It was subsequently put on in Swansea for the Taliesin Arts Centre on 24th June 2023.
19 The remaining evidence of magical interest in the Tylwyth Teg comes from manuscripts. The fairy magic in the Llyfr Cyfrin is given in the text and commentary.

Wizards, Witches and Fairies

The fairy spells in Llyfr Cyfrin differ in their focus from the Welsh folktale tradition. The spells in Llyfr Cyfrin seek to invoke (or, in modern magical parlance, evoke) the Tylwyth Teg. In the folktales the job of the dyn hysbys is always to sort out the problems that ordinary people have encountered from having the Tylwyth Teg involved in their lives. The implication is that the dyn hysbys was skilled ('hysbys') in dealing with the Tylwyth Teg, whereas the ordinary folk were out of their depth when they experienced the intervention of the Otherworld in their lives. In the folktales, the two main functions that the dyn hysbys takes care of are finding people who have been lost to the Tylwyth Teg and righting mishaps and bad luck caused by contact with the Tylwyth Teg. No one in the folktales asks the dyn hysbys to deal with the Tylwyth Teg for beneficial reasons, whereas historically both confidence tricksters and the more sincere magicians claim to call upon the Tylwyth Teg for positive advantage. This is surely to do with the nature of folktales, which are often stories about things that go wrong.

These folktale accounts are primarily stories that are not associated with named conjurors. They function primarily as entertainment or as cautionary tales.

Wales had a thriving tradition of fairy lore that is probably under-represented in the material we have. Folklore collecting came relatively late to Wales. Nineteenth-century folklore collectors outside of Wales were often outsiders, gentlefolk amateurs who had an antiquarian interest in lore.

That the folklore was chiefly in the Welsh language was a barrier to these kinds of collectors in a way that it was not to those in England or Scotland or, to a lesser extent, in Ireland. Industrialism came early to parts of Wales and this disrupted the traditional patterns of life and the folklore that accompanied them. Methodism and other forms of chapel religion were hostile to these older traditions. It was only later in the century that Welsh people were enthusiastic about their own folk traditions in their own journals. The extensive print culture of later nineteenth-century Wales is a valuable and under-researched repository of Welsh lore recorded by Welsh people who had acquired an enthusiastic antiquarian appetite for the memories and lore of previous decades. Many of the surviving accounts of dynion hysbys are to be found in the newspapers and journals that have now been digitised by the National Library of Wales.

As the Welsh language was eroded aspects of Welsh culture fell to the shore too, carried away by the tides of modernity. Thus serious folklore collection came relatively later to a country that had been changed by industrialism. Nevertheless there is a decent pot of material from which to draw and a surprising number of fairy-related tales involve the dyn hysbys or gŵr cyfarwydd or conjuror.

The following stories are presented as they occur in the original folklore collections (in their English-language versions) without a great deal of comment. Most of them are good, rollicking yarns that also contain implicit folk beliefs concerning the Tylwyth Teg and cunning folk or conjurors. The final example, from a twentieth century English storyteller, may be an invented tale that has been passed off as received tradition. These are all the Welsh stories that I could find involving fairies with magicians, conjurors, dynion and menywod hysbys, gwyr cyfarwydd and the like. I hope there are more waiting to be noticed by others.

Notable folklorists who preserved the bulk of these tales include Sir John Rhŷs (1840-1915) in *Celtic Folklore, Welsh and Manx* (1901) and Jonathan Ceredig Davies (1859-1932) in *Folk-Lore of West and Mid-Wales* (Aberystwyth, 1911)

These stories typically have a limited number of motifs, yet there are considerable differences in the settings and characters and other details. Fairies do not like to be touched with iron (although one had no probems with doing the ironing for the household). Salt may be employed. A heated shovel may be used and in one story all of these combine when salt is put upon a (presumably iron) shovel which has a cross made upon it and is heated in the fire.

In one type of story someone goes missing and the dyn hysbys is consulted. This often occurs at harvest time. The friends or relatives of the missing persons are told where they may find the fairies, who are almost always dancing in a circle with the missing person, who must be seized from the circle. Sometimes they must wait a whole year before going to the place where the fairies will appear, indicative of the way in which time passes differently with the fairies. Often the victim is no longer the same as they were before they met with the fairies and may die or disappear.

In another popular story type it is a child who is lost to the fairies and is replaced by a changeling. The mixing of pottage or a pasty in an eggshell is conducted as a way or identifying the fairies. These themes are common to fairy stories in other cultures but the prominence of the dyn hysbys in the Welsh tales is notable.

A wide range of terms is used for the dyn hysbys – gŵr cyfarwydd, gŵr cynnil, gŵr hyspys, dyn hysbys, dyn cynnil, conjuror, wise man, wizard – but not a single one is named. This may indicate that the tales have been transplanted from other locales and recontextualised. The 'parson of Trawsfynydd was skilled in the secrets of the spirits' in John Rhŷs' story about the farmer's wife of Dyffryn Mymbyr and her changeling infant is likely to be Huw Llwyd (1568-1630) of the Cynfal valley near Llan Ffestiniog.

This first tale is from a Welsh magazine from 1830, contemporary with the Llyfr Cyfrin. A man goes missing in a mysterious forest and a gŵr cyfarwydd must be consulted as to the cause and the remedy.

> In Mathavarn, in the parish of Llanwrin, and the cantrev of Cyveilioc, there is a wood which is called Ffridd yr Ywen, (the Forest of the Yew;) it is supposed to be so called, because there is a yew tree growing in the very middle of it: in many parts of this wood are to be seen green circles, which are called 'the dancing places of the goblin,' about which, a considerable time ago, the following tale was very common in the neighbourhood: Two servants of John Pugh, esq. went out, one day, to work in the 'Forest of the Yew;' pretty early in the afternoon the whole country was so covered with dark vapour, that the youths thought night was coming on; but when they came to the middle of the 'Forest," it brightened up around them, and the darkness seemed all left behind, so, thinking it too early to return home for the night, they lay down and slept. One of them, on waking, was much surprised to find no one there but himself; he wondered a good deal at the behaviour of his companion, but made up his mind, at last, that he had gone on some business of his own, as he had been talking of it some time before; so the sleeper went home, and when they inquired after his companion, he told them he was gone to the cobbler's shop. The next day they inquired of him again about his fellow-servant, but he could not give them any account of him; but at last confessed how and where they had both gone to sleep. After searching and searching many days, he went to a gŵr cyvarwydd, (a conjuror,) which was a very common trade in those days, according to the legend; and the conjuror said to him, 'Go to the same place

where you and the lad slept; go there exactly a year after the day the boy was lost; let it be on the same day of the year, and at the same time of the day: but take care that you do not step inside the fairy ring; stand on the border of the green circles you saw there, and the boy will come out, with many of the goblins, to dance; and when you see him so near to you that you may take hold of him, snatch him out of the ring as quickly as you can.' He did according to this advice, and plucked the boy out, and then asked him, 'if he did not feel hungry;' to which lie answered 'no;' for he had still the remains of his dinner that he had left in his wallet before going to sleep; and he asked 'if it was not nearly night, and time to go home,' not knowing that a year had passed by. His look was like a skeleton; and as soon as he had tasted food, he was a dead man.[1]

Fairies are famous for cooking or brewing in an eggshell, an act that is absurd for a full-size human. The eggshell occurs also in the stories set in Llanfabon and Cae Mawr, and is connected in each case with a changeling. Again, the gŵr cyfarwydd must be resorted to both to understand what is going on and to remedy it, by the horrific solution of throwing the children ino the water. Both this story and the next take place around harvest time. Elias Owen gives a very similar story which is set in Corwrion, in the fourteenth century, and an unnamed witch tells the afflicted parents to brew in an eggshell and throw the changeling twins into the water. Other versions of the story may have the eggshell and the verse but no cunning man or witch has provided advice.

In the parish of Trefeglwys, near Llanidloes, Powys, there is a little shepherd's cot, that is commonly called Twt y Cwmrws (the place of strife) on account of the extraordinary strife that has been there. The inhabitants of the cottage were a man and his wife and they had born to them twins, whom the woman nursed with great care and tenderness.

Some months afterwards indispensable business called the wife to the house of one of her nearest neighbours. Although she did not have far to go, she did not like to leave her children by themselves in their cradle, even for a minute, as her house was solitary, and there were many tales of goblins or the 'Tylwyth Têg' (the Fair Family or the Fairies) haunting the neighbourhood. However, she went and returned as soon as she could. On coming back she felt herself not a little terrified on seeing, though it was midday, some of 'the old elves of the blue petticoat,' as they are usually called; however, when she got back to her house she was rejoiced to find everything in the state she had left it.

But after some time had passed by, the good people began to wonder that the twins did not grow at all, but still continued as little dwarfs. The husband would have it that they were not his children but the woman said that they must be their children and about this arose the great strife between them that gave name to the place. One evening when the woman was very heavy of heart she determined to go and consult a Gŵr Cyfarwydd (a wise man, or a conjuror), feeling assured that everything was known to him, and he gave her his counsel. Now there was to be a harvest soon of the rye and oats, so the wise man said to her, 'When you are preparing dinner for the reapers, empty the shell of a hen's egg and boil the shell full of pottage and take it out through the door as if you meant it for a dinner to the reapers, and then listen what the twins will say. If you hear the children speaking things above the understanding of children, return into the house, take them and throw them into the waves of Llyn Ebyr, which is very near to you; but if you don't hear anything remarkable, do them no injury.'

When the day of the reaping came, the woman did as her adviser had recommended to her and as she went outside the door to listen, she heard one of the children say to the other:—

> Gwelais vesen cyn gweled derwen,
> Gwelais wy cyn gweled iâr,
> Erioed ni welais verwi bwyd i vedel,
> Mewn plisgyn wy iâr!
> Which translates as:
> Acorns before oak I knew,
> An egg before a hen,
> Never one hen's egg-shell stew,
> Enough for harvest men!

On this the mother returned to her house and took the two children and threw them into the Llyn. Suddenly the goblins in their trousers came to save their dwarves and the woman had her own children back again. Thus the strife between her and her husband ended.[2]

The parson of Trawfynydd in the next tale is probably Huw Llwyd, a preacher and poet who was a reputed wizard. The parson is specifically a conjuror, knowing the secrets of spirits. His technique for expelling the changeling is quite precise, reflecting widespread beliefs that the fairies didn't like iron, or salt. Kate Bosse-Griffiths' husband, J. Gwyn Griffiths links the use of salt here to the activities of the two spinsters in Pentre trying to prevent their brother from marrying.

Salt also had a great reputation for working wonders. Compare the story told by Evan Isaac (*Coelion Cymru*, 29-30) from Sir John Rhŷs's *Celtic Folklore* about the Fairies stealing a child and abusing it. A charm is made by a gŵr cyfarwydd to restore the child: "He made the man seek a shovel and cover it with salt and cut a cross into it. Then he put the shovel on the fire in the stranger's room, with the window open. the baby was left unattended on the doorstep."[3]

John Rhŷs credits this next tale about the farmer's wife of Dyffryn Mymbyr, near Capel Curig, and her infant to a Mr. Jones.

This woman had given birth to a healthy and vigorous child at the beginning of the harvest, one wretched and inclement summer. As the homestead was a considerable distance from church or chapel, and the weather so very rainy, it was neglected to baptize the child at the usual time, that is to say, before it was eight days old. One fine day, in the middle of this wretched harvest, the mother went to the field with the rest of the family to try to save the harvest, and left her baby sleeping in its cradle in its grandmother's charge, who was so aged and decrepit as to be unable to go much about. The old woman fell asleep, and, while she was in that state, the Tylwyth Teg came in and took away the baby, placing another in its stead. Very shortly the latter began to whine and groan, so that the grandmother awoke: she went to the cradle, where she saw a slender, wizened old man moving restlessly and peevishly about. 'Alas! alas!' said she, 'the old Tylwyth have been here'; and she at once blew in the horn to call the mother home, who came without delay. As she heard the crying in the cradle, she ran towards it, and lifted the little one without looking at him; she hugged him, put him to her breast, and sang lullaby to him, but nothing was of any avail, as he continued, without stopping, to scream enough to break her heart; and she knew not what to do to calm him. At last she looked at him: she saw that he was not like her dear little boy, and her heart was pierced with agony. She looked at him again, and the more she examined him the uglier he seemed to her. She sent for her husband home from the field, and told him to search for a skilled man gŵr cyfarwydd somewhere or other; and, after a long search, he was told by somebody that the parson of Trawsfynydd was skilled in the secrets of the spirits; so he went to him. The latter bade him take a shovel and cover it with salt, and make the figure of the cross in the salt; then to take it to the chamber where the fairy child was, and, after taking care to open the window, to place the shovel on the fire until the salt was burnt. This was done, and when the salt had got white hot, the peevish abortion went away, seen of no one, and they found the other baby whole and unscathed at the doorstep.[4]

This next brief story contains many elements of the missing person meme. There are many structural transformations: the missing person is still a servant but is now a girl, and the man who pulls her out of the circle a year later must be wearing the same clothes as he did when she disappeared. When the girl reappears she is still concerned about the calves for whom they had been searching. Once returned she is subject to the condition famous for the fairy bride of not being struck by iron.

On a certain day in spring the farmer living at ——— (Mr. Davies does not remember the name of the farm) lost his calves; and the servant man and the servant girl went out to look for them, but as they were both crossing a marshy flat, the man suddenly missed the girl. He looked for her, and as he could not see her he concluded that she was playing a trick on him. However, after much shouting and searching about the place, he began to think that she must have found her way home, so he turned back and asked if the girl had come in, when he found to his surprise that nobody had seen her come back. The news of her being lost caused great excitement in the country around, since many suspected that he had for some reason put an end to her life: some accounted for it in this way, and some in another. But as nothing could be found out about her, the servant man was taken into custody on the charge of having murdered her. He protested with all his heart, and no evidence could be produced that he had killed the girl.

Now, as some had an idea that she had gone to the fairies, it was resolved to send to 'the wise man' (Y dyn hysbys). This was done, and he found out that the missing girl was with the fairies: the trial was delayed, and he gave the servant man directions of the usual kind as to how to get her out. She was watched at the end of the period of twelve months and a day coming round in the dance in the fairy ring at the place where she was lost, and she was successfully drawn out of the ring; but the servant man had to be there in the same clothes as he had on when she left him. As soon as she was released and saw the servant she asked about the calves. On the way home she told her master, the servant man, and the others, that she would stay with them until her master should strike her with iron, but they went their way home in great joy at having found her. One day, however, when her master was about to start from home, and whilst he was getting the horse and cart ready, he asked the girl to assist him, which she did willingly; but as he was bridling the horse, the bit touched the girl and she disappeared instantly, and was never seen from that day forth.[5]

The following, often known as the Changeling of Llanfabon, is one of the most famous of Welsh fairy stories and has a wide range of motifs, including the genuine conjuring practices of using a crossroads for spirit evocation and the magical associations of the black hen without a single white feather. 'Bendith y mamu', 'the mothers' blessing,' or 'Bendith eu Mamau,' 'their mothers' blessing,' was a more common name for the fairies in south Wales.

Mr. Craigfryn Hughes has sent me another tale about the fairies: it has to do with the parish of Llanfabon, near the eastern border of Glamorganshire. Many traditions cluster round the church of Llanfabon, beginning with its supposed building by Saint Mabon, but which of the Mabons of Welsh legend he was, is not very certain. Not very far is a place called Pant y Dawns, or the Dance Hollow, in allusion to the visits paid to the spot by Bendith y Mamau, as the fairies are there called. In the same neighbourhood stand also the ruins of Castell y Nos, or the Castle of the Night, which tradition represents as uninhabitable because it had been built of stones from Llanfabon Church, and on account of the ghosts that used to haunt it.

However, one small portion of it was usually tenanted formerly by a 'wise man' or by a witch.

In fact, the whole country round Llanfabon Church teemed with fairies, ghosts, and all kinds of uncanny creatures:–

'At a farm house still remaining in the parish of Llanfabon, which is called the Berth Gron, there lived once upon a time a young widow and her infant child. After losing her husband her only comfort in her bereavement and solitary state was young Griff, her son. He was about three years old and a fine child for his age. The parish was then crammed full of Bendith y Mamau, and when the moon was bright and full they were wont to keep people awake with their music till the break of day. The fairies of Llanfabon were remarkable on account of their ugliness, and they were equally remarkable on account of the tricks they played. Stealing children from their cradles during the absence of their mothers, and luring men by means of their music into some pestilential and desolate bog, were things that seemed to afford them considerable amusement. It was no wonder then that mothers used to be daily on the watch lest they should lose their children. The widow alluded to was remarkably careful about her son, so much so, that it made some of the neighbours say that she was too anxious about him and that some misfortune would overtake her child. But she paid no attention to their words, as all her joy, her comfort, and her hopes appeared to meet together in her child.

However, one day she heard a moaning voice ascending from near the cow-house, and lest anything had happened to the cattle, she ran there in a fright, leaving the door of the house open and her little son in the cradle. Who can describe her grief on her coming in and seeing that her son was missing? She searched everywhere for him, but it was in vain. About sunset, behold a little lad made his appearance before her and said to her quite distinctly, "Mother." She looked minutely at him, and said at last, "Thou art not my child." "I am truly," said the little one. But the mother did not seem satisfied about it, nor did she believe it was her child.

Something whispered to her constantly, as it were,

that it was not her son. However, he remained with her a whole year, but he did not seem to grow at all, whereas Griff, her son, was a very growing child. Besides, the little fellow was getting uglier every day. At last she resolved to go to the "wise man," dyn hysbys in order to have information and light on the matter. There happened then to be living at Castell y Nos, "Castle of the Night," a man who was remarkable for his thorough acquaintance with the secrets of the evil one. When she had laid her business before him and he had examined her, he addressed the following remark to her: "It is a crimbil' and thy own child is with those old Bendith somewhere or other: if thou wilt follow my directions faithfully and minutely thy child will be restored to thee soon. Now, about noon tomorrow cut an egg through the middle; throw the one half away from thee, but keep the other in thy hand, and proceed to mix it backwards and forwards. See that the little fellow be present paying attention to what thou art doing, but take care not to call his attention to it—his attention must be drawn to it without calling to him—and very probably he will ask what thou wouldst be doing. Thou art to say that it is mixing a pasty for the reapers that thou art. Let me know what he will then say." The woman returned, and on the next day she followed the cunning man's advice to the letter: the little fellow stood by her and watched her minutely; presently he asked, "Mother, what are you doing?" "Mixing a pasty for the reapers, my boy."

Oh, that is it. I heard from my father—he had heard it from his father and that one from his father—that an acorn was before the oak, and that the oak was in the earth; but I have neither heard nor seen anybody mixing the pasty for the reapers in an egg-shell." The woman observed that he looked very cross as he spoke, and that it so added to his ugliness that it made him highly repulsive.

'That afternoon the woman went to the cunning man dyn cynnil in order to inform him of what the dwarf had said. "Oh," said he, "he is of that old breed; now the next full moon will be in four days—thou must go where the four roads meet above Rhyd y Gloch, at twelve o'clock the night the moon is full. Take care to hide thyself at a spot where thou canst see the ends of the crossroads; and shouldst thou see anything that would excite thee take care to be still and to restrain thyself from giving way to thy feelings, otherwise the scheme will be frustrated and thou wilt never have thy son back." The unfortunate mother knew not what to make of the strange story of the cunning man; she was in the dark as much as ever. At last the time came, and by the appointed hour she had concealed herself carefully behind a large bush close by, whence she could see everything around. She remained there a long time watching; but nothing was to be seen or heard, while the profound and melancholy silence of midnight dominated over all. At last she began to hear the sound of music approaching from afar; nearer and nearer the sweet sound continued to come, and she listened to it with rapt attention. Ere long it was close at hand, and she perceived that it was a procession of Bendith y Mamau going somewhere or other. They were hundreds in point of number, and about the middle of the procession she beheld a sight that pierced her heart and made the blood stop in her veins-walking between four of the Bendith she saw her own dear little child. She nearly forgot herself altogether, and was on the point of springing into the midst of them violently to snatch him from them if she could; but when she was on the point of leaping out of her hiding place for that purpose, she thought of the warning of the cunning man dyn cynnil, that any disturbance on her part would frustrate all, so that she would never get her child back. When the procession had wound itself past, and the sound of the music had died away in the distance, she issued from her concealment and directed her steps homewards. Full of longing as she was for her son before, she was much more so now; and her disgust at the little dwarf who claimed to be her son had very considerably grown, for she was now certain in her mind that he was one of the old breed. She knew not how to endure him for a moment longer under the same roof with her, much less his addressing her as "mother." However, she had enough restraining grace to behave becomingly towards the ugly little fellow that was with her in the house. On the morrow she went without delay to the "wise man" dyn cynnil to relate what she had witnessed the previous night, and to seek further advice. The cunning man gŵr cynnil expected her, and as she entered he perceived by her looks that she had seen something that had disturbed her.

She told him what she had beheld at the cross-roads, and when he had heard it he opened a big book which he had; then, after he had long pored over it, he told her, that before she could get her child back, it was necessary for her to find a black hen without a single white feather, or one of any other colour than black: this she was to place to bake before a wood fire with its feathers and all intact. Moreover, as soon as she placed it before the fire, she was to close every hole and passage in the walls except one, and not to look very intently after the crimbil until the hen was done enough and the feathers had fallen off it every one: then she might look where he was.

'Strange as the advice of the wise man cyfarwyddyd y 'gŵr' sounded, she resolved to try it; so she went the next day to search among the hens for one of the requisite description; but to her disappointment she failed to find one. She then walked from one farm house to another in her search; but fortune appeared to scowl at her, as she seemed to fail in her object. When, however, she was nearly disheartened, she came across the kind of hen she wanted at a farm at the end of the parish. She bought it, and after returning home she arranged the fire and killed the hen, which she placed in front of the bright fire burning on the hearth. Whilst watching the hen baking she altogether forgot the crimbil; and she fell into a sort of swoon, when she was astonished by the sound of music outside the house, similar to the music she had heard a few nights before at the crossroads. The feathers had by this time fallen off the hen, and when she came to look for the crimbil he had disappeared. The mother cast wild looks about the house, and to her joy she heard the voice of her lost son calling to her from outside. She ran to meet him, and embraced him fervently. But when she asked him where he had been so long, he had no account in the world to give but that he had been listening to pleasant music. He was very thin and worn in appearance when he was restored. Such is the story of the Lost Child.'[6]

Welsh fairies often had unusual names. Sometimes these gave a human some power or influence over the fairy. In this case it causes the fairy to leave the house. I have slightly modified the translation of the verse to make it more literal and scurrilous.

GWARWYN-A-THROT

Long ago there was in service at a Monmouthshire farm a young woman who was merry and strong. Who she was or whence she came nobody knew; but many believed that she belonged to the old breed of Bendith y Mamau. Some time after she had come to the farm, the rumour spread that the house was sorely troubled by a spirit. But the girl and the elf understood one another well, and they became the best of friends. So the elf proved very useful to the maid, for he did everything for her – washing, ironing, spinning and twisting wool; in fact they say that he was remarkably handy at the spinning-wheel. Moreover, he expected only a bowlful of sweet milk and wheat bread, or some flummery, for his work. So she took care to place the bowl with his food at the bottom of the stairs every night as she went to bed. It ought to have been mentioned that she was never allowed to catch a sight of him; for he always did his work in the dark. Nor did anybody know when he ate his food: she used to leave the bowl there at night, and it would be empty by the time when she got up in the morning, the bwca having cleared it. But one night, by way of cursedness, what did she do but fill the bowl with some of the stale urine which they used in dyeing wool and other things about the house. But heavens! it would have been better for her not to have done it; for when she got up next morning what should he do but suddenly spring from some corner and seize her by the neck! He began to beat her and kick her from one end of the house to the other, while he shouted at the top of his voice at every kick:–

Y faidan din dwmp–
Yn rhoi bara haidd a thrwnc
I'r bwca!

The idea that the fat-bottomed lass
Should give barley bread and piss
To the pwca!

Meanwhile she screamed for help, but none came for some time; when, however, he heard the servant men getting up, he took to his heels as hard as he could; and nothing was heard of him for some time. But at the end of two years he was found to be at another farm in the neighbourhood, called Hafod yr Ynys, where he at once became great friends with the servant girl: for she fed him like a young chicken, by giving him a little bread and milk all the time. So he worked willingly and well for her in return for his favourite food. More especially, he used to spin and wind the yarn for her; but she wished him in time to show his face, or to tell her his name: he would by no means do either. One evening, however, when all the men were out, and when he was spinning hard at the wheel, she deceived him by telling him that she was also going out. He believed her; and when he heard the door shutting, he began to sing as he plied the wheel:–

Hi wardda'n iawn pe gwypa hi,
Taw Gwarwyn-a-throt yw'm enw i.

How she would laugh, did she know
That Gwarwyn-a-throt is my name!

'Ha! ha!' said the maid at the bottom of the stairs; 'I know thy name now.' 'What is it, then?' he asked. She replied, 'Gwarwyn-a-throt'; and as soon as she uttered the words he left the wheel where it was, and off he went.

He was next heard of at a farmhouse not far off, where there happened to be a servant man named Moses, with whom he became great friends at once. He did all his work for Moses with great ease. He once, however, gave him a good beating for doubting his word; but the two remained together afterwards for some years on the best possible terms: the end of it was that Moses became a soldier. He went away to fight against Richard Crookback, and fell on the field of Bosworth. The bogie, after losing his friend, began to be troublesome and difficult to live with. He would harass the oxen when they ploughed, and draw them after him everywhere, plough and all; nor could any one prevent them. Then, when the sun set in the evening he would play his pranks again, and do all sorts of mischief about the house, upstairs, and in the cowhouses. So the farmer was advised to visit a wise man (dyn cynnil), and to see if he could devise some means of getting rid of the bogie. He called on the wise man, who happened to be living near Caerleon on the Usk; and the wise man, having waited till the moon should be full, came to the farmer's house. In due time the wise man, by force of manœuvring, secured the bogie by the very long nose which formed the principal ornament of his face, and earned for him the name of Bwca'r Trwyn, 'the Bogie of the Nose.' Whilst secured by the nose, the bogie had something read to him out of the wise man's big book; and he was condemned by the wise man to be transported to the banks of the Red Sea for fourteen generations, and to be conveyed thither by 'the upper wind' (yr uwchwynt). No sooner had this been pronounced by the cunning man than there came a whirlwind which made the whole house shake. Then came a still mightier wind, and as it began to blow the owner of the big book drew the awl out of the bogie's nose; and it is supposed that the bogie was carried away by that wind, for he never troubled the place any more.[7]

In this next tale it is turfcutters who sit in a circle. One of them has washed his face in a fairy well and when he leaves the circle to fetch food he disappears.

Rather than during harvest the story is set at a full moon in June.

> The scene was a turbary near the river called Afon Mynach, so named from Cwm Tir Mynach, behind the hills immediately north of Bala: – Ages ago, as a number of people were cutting turf in a place which was then moorland, and which is now enclosed ground forming part of a farm called Nant Hir, one of them happened to wash his face in a well belonging to the fairies. At dinner-time in the middle of the day they sat down in a circle, while the youth who had washed his face went to fetch the food, but suddenly both he and the box of food were lost. They knew not what to do, they suspected that it was the doing of the fairies; but the wise man (gŵr hyspys) came to the neighbourhood and told them, that, if they would only go to the spot on the night of full moon in June, they would behold him dancing with the fairies. They did as they were told, and found the moor covered with thousands of little agile creatures who sang and danced with all their might, and they saw the missing man among them. They rushed at him, and with a great deal of trouble they got him out. But oftentimes was Einion missed again, until at the time of full moon in another June he returned home with a wondrously fair wife, whose history or pedigree no one knew. Everybody believed her to be one of the Tylwyth Teg.[8]

According to John Rhŷs this derives from 'Mr. B. Davies in the II. Vol. of the "Brython," page 182'. It is a version of the changeling story that is now set in in the area of Newcastle Emlyn. The fairies are Plant Rhŷs Ddwfn, the Children of Deep Rhŷs, The remedy involves a red hot shovel alone and it is held before the changeling's face, suggesting the threat of violence.

> One calm hot day, when the sun of heaven was brilliantly shining, and the hay in the dales was being busily made by lads and lasses, and by grown-up people of both sexes, a woman in the neighbourhood of Emlyn placed

her one-year-old infant in the 'gader' or chair, as the cradle is called in these parts, and out she went to the field for a while, intending to return when her neighbour, an old woman overtaken by the decrepitude of eighty summers, should call to her that her Darling was crying. It was not long before she heard the old woman calling to her; she ran hurriedly, and as soon as she set foot on the kitchen floor, she took her little one in her arms as usual, saying to him, 'O my little one! thy mother's delight art thou! I would not take the world for thee, etc.' But to her surprise, he had a very old look about him, and the more the tender-hearted mother gazed at his face, the stranger it seemed to her, so that at last she placed him in the cradle and told her sorrow to her relatives and acquaintances. And after this one and the other had given his opinion, it was agreed at last that it was one of Rhys Ddwfn's children that was in the cradle, and not her dearly loved baby. In this distress there was nothing to do but to fetch a wizard, or wise man, as fast as the fastest horse could gallop. He said, when he saw the child that he had seen his like before, and that it would be a hard job to get rid of him, though not such a very hard job this time. The shovel was made red hot in the fire by one of the Cefnarth (Cenarth) boys, and held before the child's face; and in an instant the short little old man took to his heels, and neither he nor his like was seen afterwards from Abercuch to Aberbargod at any rate. The mother found her darling unscathed the next moment. I remember also hearing that the strange child was as old as the grandfather of the one that had been lost.[9]

The following is the single story that breaks my rule about the dyn hysbys or conjuror being unnamed. It is included here because it is a clear example of a missing person tale.

One of Mr. Roberts' tales is in point: he had it from Mr. Hugh Francis, of Holyhead House, Ruthin, and the latter heard it from Robert Roberts, of Amlwch, who has now been dead about thirty years:–About 105 years ago there lived in the parish of Llandyfrydog, near Llannerch y Medd, in Anglesey, a man named Ifan Gruffydd, whose cow happened to disappear one day. Ifan Gruffydd was greatly distressed, and he and his daughter walked up and down the whole neighbourhood in search of her. As they were coming back in the evening from their unsuccessful quest, they crossed the field called after the Dyfrydog thief, Cae Lleidr Dyfrydog, where they saw a great number of little men on ponies quickly galloping in a ring. They both drew nigh to look on; but Ifan Gruffydd's daughter, in her eagerness to behold the little knights more closely, got unawares within the circle in which their ponies galloped, and did not return to her father. The latter now forgot all about the loss of the cow, and spent some hours in searching for his daughter; but at last he had to go home without her, in the deepest sadness. A few days afterwards he went to Mynaddwyn to consult John Roberts, who was a magician of no mean reputation. That 'wise man' told Ifan Gruffydd to be no longer sad, since he could get his daughter back at the very hour of the night of the anniversary of the time when he lost her. He would, in fact, then see her riding round in the company of the Tylwyth Teg whom he had seen on that memorable night. The father was to go there accompanied by four stalwart men, who were to aid him in the rescue of his daughter. He was to tie a strong rope round his waist, and by means of this his friends were to pull him out of the circle when he entered to seize his daughter. He went to the spot, and in due time he beheld his daughter riding round in great state. In he rushed and snatched her, and, thanks to his friends, he got her out of the fairy ring before the little men had time to think of it. The first thing Ifan's daughter asked him was, if he had found the cow, for she had not the slightest reckoning of the time she had spent with the fairies.[10]

This next story breaks the mould and is the last one from John Rhŷs. The intervention of a 'wise man' is threatened but not enacted and the changeling is believed to be swapped by a witch who communes annually with fairies, bendith eu mamau, in a cave and offers them human children that she replaces with changelings for payment of gold.

There was formerly an old woman living in a small house near Ynys Geinon; and she had the power of bewitching, people used to say: there was a rumour that she spent seven days, seven hours, and seven minutes with the fairies every year in the cave at the Castle. It was a pretty general belief that she got such and such a quantity of gold for every child she could steal for them, and that she put one of those old urchins of theirs in its place: the latter never grew at all. The way she used to do it was to enter people's houses with the excuse of asking for alms, having a large dark-grey old cloak on her back, and the cloak concealed one of the children of Bendith eu Mamau. Whenever she found the little child of the good woman of the house in its cradle, she would take upon herself to rock the cradle, so that if the mother only turned her back for a minute or two, she would throw the sham child into the cradle and hurry away as fast as she could with the baby. A man in the neighbourhood had a child lingering for years without growing at all, and it was the opinion of all that it had been changed by the old woman. The father at length threatened to call in the aid of "the wise man," when the old woman came there for seven days, pretending that it was in order to bathe the little boy in cold water; and on the seventh day she got permission to take him, before it was light, under a certain spout of water: so she said, but the neighbours said it was to change him. However that was, the boy from that time forth got on as fast as a gosling. But the mother had all but to take an oath to the old woman, that she would duck him in cold water every morning for three months, and by the end of that time there was no finer infant in the Cwm.[11]

These tales included by J. Ceredig Davies are worth including for their minor variations in storytelling, but are each versions of the missing person/fairy circle theme.

A FARM SERVANT NEAR TREGARON, WHO SPENT A YEAR AND A DAY WITH THE FAIRIES.

The following story appeared in 'Cymru' for May, 1893, a Welsh Magazine, edited by Owen M. Edwards, M.A. It was written in Welsh by the late eminent Folk-Lorist, Mr. D. Lledrod Davies, and I translate it:—

The farm-house called 'Allt Ddu,' is situated about half-way between Pont Rhyd Fendigaid and Tregaron.

It is said that two servant men went out of the house one evening in search for the cattle, which had gone astray. One of the men proceeded in one direction and the other in another way, so as to be more sure of finding the animals.

But after wandering about for hours, one of the two servants came home, but whether he found the cattle or not it is not stated. However, he reached home safely; but the other man, his fellow-servant, came not, and after anxiously expecting him till a late hour of night, he began to feel very uneasy concerning his safety, fearing that the lad had accidentally fallen into some of the pits of the Gors Goch. Next morning came, but the servant came not home; and in vain did they long to hear the sound of his footsteps approaching the house as before.

Then inquiries were made about him, and people went to try and find him, but all in vain. Days past and even weeks without hearing anything about him, till at last his relations began to suspect that his fellow servant had murdered him during the night they were out looking for the cattle. So the servant was summoned before a Court of Justice, and accused of having murdered his fellow-servant on a certain night; but the young man, pleaded not guilty in a most decided manner, and as no witness could be found against him, the case was dismissed; but many people were still very suspicious of him, and the loss of his fellow servant continued to be a black spot on his character. However, it was decided at last to go to the 'dyn hysbys,' (a wise man, or a conjuror)—a man of great repute in former days, – to consult with him, and to set the case before him exactly as it had happened. After going and explaining everything to the conjuror concerning the lost servant, he informed them that the young man was still alive.

He then told them to go to a certain place at the same time of night, one year and a day from the time the man was lost, and that they should then and there see him. One year and a day at last passed away, and at that hour the family, and especially the servant, traced their steps to the particular spot pointed out by the conjuror, and there, to their great surprise, whom should they see within the Fairy Circle, dancing as merrily as any, but the lost servant. And now, according to the directions which had been given by the conjuror, the other servant took hold of the collar of the coat of the one who was dancing, and dragged him out of the circle, saying to him – 'Where hast thou been lad?' But the lad's first words were, 'Did you find the cattle?' for he thought that he had been with the Fairies only for a few minutes.

Then he explained how he entered the Fairy Circle, and how he was seized by them, but found their company so delightful that he thought he had been with them only for a few minutes.[12]

THE SERVANT GIRL WHO WAS LOST IN THE FAIRY CIRCLE.

The following is another of the tales recorded in 'Ystraeon y Gwyll,' by the late D. Lledrod Davies: –

'There lived in an old farm house on the banks of the Teivy, a respectable family, and in order to carry on the work of the farm successfully, they kept men servants and maid servants.

One afternoon, a servant-man and a servant girl went out to look for the cows, but as they were both crossing a marshy flat, the man suddenly missed the girl, and after much shouting and searching, no sound of her voice could be heard replying. He then took home the cows, and informed the family of the mysterious disappearance of the servant maid which took place so suddenly. As the Fairies were suspected, it was resolved to go to the dyn hysbys (wise man).

To him they went, and he informed them that the girl was with the Fairies, and that they could get her back from them, by being careful to go to a certain spot at the proper time at the end of a year and a day. They did as they were directed by the "wise man," and to their great surprise, found the maid among the fairies dancing and singing with them, and seemed as happy as a fish in the water. Then they successfully drew her out of the ring, and they took her home safely. The master had been told by the "Wise Man" that the girl was not to be touched by iron, or she would disappear at once after getting her out of the ring.

One day, however, when her master was about to start from home, and whilst he was getting the horse and cart ready, he asked the girl to assist him, which she did willingly; but as he was bridling the horse, the bit touched the girl and she disappeared instantly, and was never seen from that day forth.'[13]

A MAN WHO WAS FOUND AMONG THE FAIRIES AT CAE CEFN PANTY-DWR.

A certain man of Llanedi, on one occasion long ago, went away to another neighbourhood, leading by the 'penwast' (collar) a very wild and unmanageable horse; and in order to be sure not to lose his hold of the animal, the man tied the end of the collar round the middle. So both man and horse went together and got lost. After much searching the horse was found without the collar, but nothing was heard of the man. After giving up searching for him as hopeless, they at last consulted a 'Dyn Hysbys,' (a conjuror or a wise man). The wise man directed them to go on a certain night into a field known as Cae Cefn Pantydwr, about forty yards from the road where the Fairies could be seen dancing, and the lost man among them, with the 'penwast' still around his waist, which would enable them to know him; and the way to get him out of the Fairy Ring was to watch him coming round in the dance, and take hold of the collar when an opportunity offered itself, and drag the man out boldly. They did so, and the man was rescued. Ever since then people dreaded going to that field after dark, especially children.[14]

This story is included in *The Welsh Fairy Book*, p. 163-166 as 'Getting Rid of the Fairies'. *The Welsh Fairy Book* is an often unreliable collection that nevertheless has well-told stories and became the most popular modern source for Welsh tales. This story is unusually specific in its setting, containing many place names, even the name of Morgan Rhys' farm. Neither the wise woman of Penderyn nor the 'cunning man of great reputation' of Pentre Felyn are identifiable. The 'wise woman' and 'cunning man' were obviously Jenkyn's own additions, perhaps inspired by the dyn hysbys in the Llanfabon Changeling story. Morgan Rhys seem unrelated to Morgan ap Rhys who had a fairy harp.[15] Jenkyns also combines other tales together to make the versions that are familiar today. Another example mentioned in this book is that of Bela Fawr who is made into one of the Llanddona witches.

Dewi Dal was a farmer, whose house was over-run with fairies, so that he could not sleep of nights for the noise they made. Dewi consulted a wise man of Taiar, who entrusted Dewi's wife to do certain things, which she did carefully, as follows: 'It was the commencement of oat harvest, when Cae Mawr, or the big field, which it took fifteen men to mow in a day, was ripe for the harvesters. "I will prepare food for the fifteen men who are going to mow Cae Mawr to-morrow," said Eurwallt, the wife, aloud. "Yes, do," replied Dewi, also aloud, so that the fairies might hear, "and see that the food is substantial and sufficient for the hard work before them." Said Eurwallt, "The fifteen men shall have no reason to complain upon that score. They shall be fed according to our means." Then when evening was come Eurwallt prepared food for the harvesters' sustenance upon the following day. Having procured a sparrow, she trussed it like a fowl, and roasted it by the kitchen fire. She then placed some salt in a nut-shell, and set the sparrow and the salt, with a small piece of bread, upon the table, ready for the fifteen men's support while mowing Cae Mawr. So when the fairies beheld the scanty provision made for so many men, they said "Let us quickly depart from this place, for alas! the means of our hosts are exhausted. Who before this was ever so reduced in circumstances as to serve up a sparrow for the day's food of fifteen men?" So they departed upon that very night. And Dewi Dal and his family lived, ever afterwards, in comfort and peace.'

Ruth Tongue (1898-1981) was an English storyteller and folklorist who was linked with rural Somerset, to which she moved in the 1950s. She was a friend of Katherine Briggs (1898-1980), a renowned folklorist who pioneered the serious study of fairy folklore in Britain and Ireland and published a mammoth compendium of the *Folk Tales of Britain* in six volumes. Ruth Tongue related a story set in the Welsh marches in which a young man ineptly conjures a fairy and suffers the consequences for the rest of his life.

THE FAIRY FOLLOWER

There was once a lad, and he loved a girl with all his heart, and all he wanted was to marry her. His love was so hot that he could not bear to wait, but set to to get help from the fairies. It was an un-chancy thing to do, and he set about it the wrong way. First, he took a fair white cloth without asking the farmer's wife's leave, and no good could come of that. Then he filled a pail of river-water, and that wouldn't do. Then he tried a pail of well-water, and that wouldn't do. At last he filled a pail of clear spring-water, and that was right enough, but he stood it outside the door on the night of the new moon, instead of inside, so nothing came of that. So he had to wait a whole month, till the next new moon, and for two nights running he set the pail inside the door, but that wasn't good enough, and still nothing happened. So he waited another month; it was May by this time, and he swept the hearth, and put the pail of water to stand on it, two nights before the new moon, and that was right. Just after midnight, he tiptoed down to the pail, and there was a thin gold film on top of the water. He skimmed it off, and made a cake of it, with meal, and set it down on the fair white cloth. He made a circle, and said the words, and waited.

The door opened, and a dark fairy came in, and stretched out her hand for the cake.

'Not for thee,' he said, and he shouldn't have spoken.

Then a fair fairy came in, and stretched out her hand. He tapped her on the wrist and said, 'Not for thee.' But he shouldn't have touched her.

Then came a most beautiful lady in green, and she said, 'For me,' and ate the cake.

After that she was always with him, and he told her his wishes. She granted them right enough, but in a back-handed way that turned them all to bitterness. He wanted marriage, and he got it, but with a cruel old woman, the richest in the parish. So he had his money too, and small good it did him. Then a great pestilence came on the place, and people died to the right and left of him, and his poor pretty sweet heart, whom he had loved all his life, was the first to die, but the lad's great strength bore him through everything, and it seemed he could not die. But at length the fairy at his elbow, meddling and urging him this way and that, though no one else could see her, wore him down to a thread, and he died. As he lay in his coffin, a dark, cloudy shadow came down over it, and out of the darkness a voice said, very cold and clear, 'For me.'[16]

Katherine Briggs' summary of the story in The Fairies in Tradition and Literature brings out the elements of the tale more successfully than the verbatim version included in *Folk Tales of Britain*.

> ... The Fairy Follower, a tale from the Welsh Marches, heard by R. L. Tongue in the 1920s. It is of a young man

who was deeply in love, and was too impatient to wait and work for his sweetheart; so he tried to obtain a fairy helper. The method he used was very like that described in a seventeenth-century magical manuscript, setting out clear water for the fairies, and afterwards preparing a meal of bread and cheese for them; but he made various blunders in the preparations and procedure, and, though he procured the fairy and she promised to grant his wishes, she did so in a back-handed way that broke his heart. He got his wife and riches, but it was a cross old rich woman he found himself married to instead of his sweetheart, who died in an epidemic through which his great strength carried him unhurt. And the fairy was always by his side, prompting him and giving him no peace; till at length he died of a broken heart, and as he lay on his hearse a cold, clear voice claimed his soul for its own. There is clearly little distinction between this fairy and a devil.[17]

Ruth Tongue's work in folklore has been roundly criticised for not representing actual folk tradition. My general impression is that she was primarily a storyteller who happily retold material she found from many sources, including published collections of folklore, while passing it off as material she had found in the oral tradition. We might compare her to Iolo Morganwg who invented huge swathes of Welsh lore, or to Glasynys who blithely told new stories using the names of Welsh legendary characters like Taliesin.[18]

It is notable that this tale is said to come from 'the Welsh marches', a vague designation which could cover any region on the border between Wales and England, rather than from a specific village, town or even county.

Briggs recognises the similarity between the seventeenth-century spell which she herself published and Tongue's tale.

The following is the spell Briggs is comparing to Ruth Tongue's. I have modernised the spelling without changing the English in any other way.

'Experimentum optimum verissimum for the fairies."

In the night before the new moon, or the same night, or the night after the new moon, or else the night before the full moon, the night of the full, or the night after the full moon, go to the house where the fairies maids do use and provide you a fair and clean bucket, or pail clean washed, with clear water therein and set it by the chimney side or where fire is made, and having a fair new towel or one clean washed by, and so depart till the morning; then be thou the first that shall come to the bucket or water before the sun rise, and take it to the light, that you find upon the water a white rime, like raw milk or grease, take it by with a silver spoon, and put it into a clean saucer; then the next night following come to the same house again before 11 of the clock at night, making a good fire with sweet woods and set upon the table a new towel or one clean washed and upon it 3 fine loaves of new mangett fine wheat bread, 3 new knives with white hafts and a new cup full of new ale, then set your self down by the fire in a chair with your face towards the table and anoint your eyes with the same cream or oil aforesaid.

Then you shall see come by you three fair maids, and as they pass by they will obey you with becking their heads to you, and like as they do to you, so do you to them, but say nothing. Suffer the first, whatsoever she be, to pass, for she is malignant, but to the second or third as you like best reach forth your hand and pluck her to you, and with few words ask her when she will appoint a place to meet you the next morning for to assoyle such questions as you will demand of her; and then, if she will grant you, suffer her to depart and go to her company till the hour appointed, but miss her not at the time and place; then will the other, in the mean time while you are talking with her, go to the table and eat of that is there, then will they depart from you, and as they obey you, do you the like to them saying nothing, but letting them depart quietly. Then when your hour is come to meet, say to her your mind, for then will she come alone. Then covenant with her for all matters convenient for your purpose and she will be always with you, of this assure yourself for it is proved, ffinis the end.[19]

In the spell a clean bucket with clear water on the night of the new or full moon, or one night before or after must be placed by a chimney. The first to come to the bucket before the sun has risen will find a white rime on the water that should be placed onto a saucer with a silver spoon.

In Ruth Tongue's story there are three attempts to obtain the rime from the bucket of clear water. First river-water is tried, then well-water, then it is spring-water that is successful. These three attempt mirror the three fairy women who will appear.

In the spell this rime would be used to anoint the eyes, and bread and ale are placed on a towel. In Ruth tongue's story the rime is used to make a cake with meal which is placed on a white cloth.

In the spell, the first maid to appear is malign, but it is up to the magician whether he chooses the second or third maid to assist him.

Throughout Ruth Tongue's tale the young man makes mistakes of which no good or nothing will come, and says or does things which he 'shouldn't have…'

It seems quite likely that Tongue invented a folktale-style story based on the spell that her friend Katherine Briggs had recently published. The spell and the tale provide a perfect illustration of the contrast between actual magic and folktale magic. The spell is concerned with compelling fairies to aid the magician 'for all matters convenient to your purpose…' Tongue's story is about a man who makes mistakes at all stages of the spell and suffers the consequences. The same division is found throughout Welsh fairy magic: the rituals and the historical accounts and the folklore attached to specific dynion hysbys are concerned with the magician compelling the fairies in the manner that magicians deal with spirits in general; the folktales are concerned with things that go wrong for ordinary people who must call in conjurors to help them out. However, Tongue's tale is unusual in having the protaganist as an amateur magician. If he had called in a Welsh dyn hysbys everything would have been sorted out in the end.

Notes

1 *The Cambrian Quarterly Magazine and Celtic Repertory* No. 5 January 1 1830 p.58-59
2 Elias Owen, *Welsh Folklore* 54-55. Owen found the story in *The Cambrian Magazine* ii 86-87 .
3 'A Charm to Prevent Love' in *Heddiw* 6. 1941, 177-178 See https://britishfairies.wordpress.com/2020/11/22/fairies-and-salt/ for further instances of salt being used to protect against fairies
4 John Rhŷs *Celtic Folklore Welsh and Manx* p. 100-103
5 Ibid p. 248, Welsh removed where it was duplicated in English.
6 Ibid p.257. The changeling of Llanfabon story was followed immediately by a version of the tale which is among the most famous in Wales. This is the one in which a cunning man asks a young man if he wishes to see something curious. He is led to a secret cave in which King Arthur sleeps with his men. This is clearly a version of the Otherworld, seen from a different perspective. Rhŷs gives the story on p. 462ff in the chapter about cave legends, but explains that he received it as part of a sequence of tales.
7 Ibid., p. 595-596.
8 Ibid., p. 150-151
9 Ibid., p. 161-2
10 Ibid., p. 239-240
11 Ibid., p. 256
12 *Folk-Lore of West and Mid-Wales* by Jonathan Ceredig Davies p. 108
13 Ibid., p. 109-110
14 Ibid., p. 111.
15 I'm grateful to Dr Delyth Badder for pointing out on Twitter that 'It's an amalgamation of two stories which you can find in Sikes's British Goblins–one based in Dolgellau and one in south Wales, based on an article from The Principality newspaper.' https://twitter.com/delythbadder/status/1594947471498780673
16 Katherine Briggs, *Folk Tales of Britain Legends* I p. 353-354
17 Ibid., p. 71-72
18 See, for instance https://writinginmargins.weebly.com/ruth-tongue.html
https://writinginmargins.weebly.com/home/dwarves-riddles-

and-talking-trees-how-ruth-tongue-used-famous-literature
19 https://britishfairies.wordpress.com/2020/05/31/summoning-faeries-spells-and-practices/
Published in Katherine Briggs *The Anatomy of Puck* (Routledge & Paul, 1959) p.115-116.

The Seven Sisters Spell

The spell for summoning the seven sisters of the Tylwyth Teg which opens Llyfr Cyfrin is probably the most attractive and fascinating in the notebook. Seven fairy sisters are named, along with their rulers Oberion and Micob, who must first be called upon to command the sisters, who themselves have legions . A feast that includes roast chicken and drinks is to be laid out for them on a tablecloth. Beneath this simple yet mysterious ritual lies a wealth of magical tradition that stretches through time and space for centuries in Europe and beyond.

The broad features of the ritual are defined by what has been called a table rite and by the names of the entities that are summoned. Both the practitioner and the ritual area should be clean. A circle must be outlined on the ground. A roast chicken, a bowl of water and half a pint of cream should be prepared. A light white cloth is placed over a table.

The table rite has an extensive history. In the *Fourth Book of Occult Philosophy*, ascribed traditionally to Cornelius Agrippa, a ritual is described.

> There is another kinde of Spirits which we have spoken of in the third book of Occult Philosophy, not so hurtful,

and neerest men; so also, that they are affected with humane passions, and do joy in the conversation of men, and freely do inhabit with them: and others do dwell in the Woods and Desarts...[1]

The spirits that are summoned are not specifically fairies but are clearly akin to them. The direction to place the table within the circle is close to that in Llyfr Cyfrin.

> Lastly, when you would invocate these kinde of Spirits, you ought to prepare a Table in the place of invocation, covered with clean linen; whereupon you shall set new bread, and running water or milk in new earthen vessels, and new knives. And you shall make a fire, whereupon a perfume shall be made. But let the Invocant go unto the head of the Table, and round about it let there be seats placed for the Spirits, as you please, and the Spirits being called, you shall invite them to drink and eat. But if perchance you shall fear any evil Spirit, then draw a Circle about it, and let that part of the Table at which the Invocant sits, be within the Circle, and the rest of the Table without the Circle.'[2]

The entire *Fourth Book of Occult Philosophy* along with its attendant texts such as *Heptameron* was translated into Welsh and published in *Seryddiaeth* in 1832. Thus it we know of at least four versions of the table ritual (Llyfr Dewiniaeth, Testunau Swyngyfaredd, Llyfr Cyfrin, *Seryddiaeth*) that were known in Wales in the early nineteenth century.

There were extensive national or regional variations on the contents of the feast that is provided for the fairies or spirits. As Dan Harms commented, these aren't the result of a literary relationship. A German rite set up

> a tiny table with honey, bread, butter, water and wine, atop a green hill in a pleasant setting, with the bloody sacrifice of a hen or pigeon, the blood of which is scat-

tered to various directions.[3]

The other Welsh versions of the seven sisters spell, along with their English source, offer ale and sack (sherry) to the sisters.

The dyn hysbys of Llyfr Cyfrin left these out–perhaps suggesting that he was teetotal, or that he felt it unwise to offer alcohol to spirits–and his fairies were clearly happy enough with roast chicken, and only cream and some fresh water to wash it down.[4]

The spell appeals to Micob and Oberion to send seven sisters who themselves have many legions of serving spirits. This is a common pattern in grimoire magic in which beings higher in the scheme of things are initially called upon in order to give the magician authority over the beings lower in the hierarchy who will actually communicate with the magician and will do the work or delegate it to other spirits.

The named fairy figures in the spell are equally interesting. The spelling of Oberion is consistent throughout, but his partner is spelled Meiob, Miscob and Meicob.[5]

Dan Harms has shown that the

> 'lady to the queen' appears in the seventeenth century manuscript Sloane 1727, just after a list of four names of spirits assigned to 'treasures of the earth': Florella, Mical, Tytan, and Mabb. At least three of these names are referred to elsewhere as fairy queens – Tytan being a variant of Titania, and Mical and Mabb turning up in the magical literature at various points.

Titania and Mab, like Oberion or Oberon, are familiar from Shakespeare. Micol was called into a crystal by Ellen Evans daughter of John Evans (see the chapter on the Tylwyth Teg and magicians.) Thus she has a long history of involvement with Welsh magicians.

In the same Sloane MS 1727 A spirit called 'Micol' who is 'queen of the pygmies' can be summoned via a Latin incantation beginning, "Micol o tumicoll regina pigmeorum deus Abraham: deus Isaac: deus Jacob...".

In one text Micob's appearance is described as follows,

> Nonetheless, she appears as an unnumbered entry at the end of the main list, suggesting that she sits apart from the rest. Mycob is said to appear as a meek lady dressed in green and wearing a crown. She provides a ring that gives invisibility and teaches medicine and the natural magic that lies within trees, herbs, and stones. She has seven followers – variants on those given in Sloane MS. 3824 – who perform many of the same functions. The nineteenth century occultists John Palmer and Frederick Hockley, both of whom had contact with the manuscript, copied this material for their own purposes, indicating that its influence extended even to their times. The same fairy turns up earlier in the manuscript, in a ritual to acquire a ring of invisibility. The magician draws a circle used for operations of love on the day and hour of Jupiter – an unusual combination, as Venus is typically the planet of love. After doing so, he calls upon three spirits, Micol, Titam (Titania, once again) and Burfex, to appear. The spirits appear, lay a rich table, and offer the magician wine. To acquire the ring, the magician must be prepared to kiss the most beautiful member of their company.[6]

The seven sisters of the spell have an even longer and more complex history. The appeal for the help of the seven sisters for purposes from preventing fevers to finding treasure was spread widely over Europe, from Scandinavia to Britain to Italy.

The names have changed continually from one context to another. The list of seven sisters in *Book of Treasure Spirits* is typical for early modern English manuscripts and runs Lilia, Rostilia, Foca, Folla, Africa, Julia, Venulla.

Beyond the early modern use of the seven sisters they may be found in fever charms. Kate Bosse-Griffiths noticed this in *Byd y Dyn Hysbys*, and cites a Latin charm by way of comparison. Angelika H. Rüdiger goes on to show two other charms also from Scandinavia.[7]

By the fifteenth century a charm lists the names of seven sisters. These seven sisters eventually were understood to be fairies or were akin to fairies. They lost their association with fevers and were appealed to for tasks such as treasure hunting.

Dan Harms provides a simple summary writing,

> as 'sibyls' or 'virgins.' Another group of female spirits with a long pedigree is the seven sisters, whose names are Lilia, Restilia, Foca, Fola, Afryca, Julia, and Venulia, or variations thereon. These figures, or those with similar names, appear as "fevers" in charms as early as the eleventh century. Within ritual magic texts of the sixteenth and seventeenth century, however, they are usually called upon to help the magician acquire treasure.[8]

The picture that emerges from the available evidence is as follows: there was a tradition of appealing to various religious powers to repel fevers, including the Seven Sleepers of Ephesus, who were seven Christian saints. (The seven sleepers appear a couple of times in early modern Welsh charms against gout and to aid sleeping.) So, we have fever charms, initially deploying many figures including the seven sleepers. Then we have the seven sisters as being responsible for the fevers. Then the sisters are invoked for purposes such as treasure hunting and, eventually, for any purpose.

Kate Bosse-Griffiths tried to argue that both Sibli and Julia were known in Welsh folktale fairy lore. The proximity of Affritia and Julia in the list of sisters is mirrored suggestively in a Welsh fairy name Jili Ffrwtan.

In her recent doctoral thesis Angelike Rüdiger has responded that it is unlikely that Jili Ffrwtan and the Sibi who promised to marry a lad of Braich-y-Ddinas have entered Welsh tradition via the seven sisters fairy magic spells. There is still something suggestive about the conjunction of Jili Ffrwtan and Affritia Julia.⁹

Sibi was also the name of a fairy in a version of the fairy bride tale:-

> In old times – but, for the matter of that, when she was a young woman – there were a great many of the fair family living in certain caves in the Foel from Cwm Strallyn down to the upper part of Pennant. This Tylwyth was much handsomer than any seen in any other part of the country. In point of stature they were much bigger than the ordinary ones, fair of complexion beyond everybody, with hair that was as light as flax, and eyes that were of a clear blue colour. They showed themselves in one spot or another, engaged in playing, singing, and jollity every light night. The sound of their singing used to draw the lads and the young women to look at them; and, should they be of clear complexion, the fairies would chat with them; but they would let no person of a dark hue come near them: they moved away from such a one. Now the young man of Braich y Dinas was a handsome, vigorous, and lively stripling of fair, clear, and attractive complexion. He was very fond of looking at the fair family, and had a chat with some of them often, but chiefly with one of the damsels, who surpassed all the rest in beauty and good sense. The result of frequently meeting was that they fell in love with one another, but she would not marry him. She promised, however, to go to service to him, and agreed to meet him at Pant y–I have forgotten the rest of the name – the day after, as it would not do for her to go with him while the others happened to be looking on. So he went up the next day to the Foel, and the damsel met him according to her promise, and went with him home, where she took to the duties of a dairymaid. Soon everything began to prosper under her hand; the butter and the cheese were daily growing in quantity. Long and importunately did the youth try to get her to marry him. She promised to do so provided he could find out her name. Mrs. Roberts did not know by what manœuvre he succeeded in discovering it, but it was done, and he came

into the house one night and called to "Sibi," and when she heard her name she fainted away. When, however, she recovered her consciousness, she consented to marry on the condition that he was not to touch her with iron, and that there was not to be a bolt of iron on the door, or a lock either. It was agreed, and they were married; they lived together comfortably many years, and had children born to them. The end came thus: he had gone one day to cut a bundle of rushes for thatching, and planted the reaping-hook in the bundle to go home. As he drew towards the haggard, Sibi ran out to meet him, and he wantonly threw the bundle of rushes towards her, when she, to prevent its hitting her, tried to stop it with her hand, which touched the reaping-hook. She vanished on the spot out of sight behind the bundle of rushes, and nothing more was seen or heard of her.[10]

Llyfr Cyfrin is unique in giving the name Sibia to the first of the sisters. In the Ellis Edwart version, in Sloane MS 3824 (*Book of Treasure Spirits*) and elsewhere the first sister is named Ilia or Illia. Sibylla is the name of a fairy that is summoned with her two sisters in Reginald Scott. One spell takes place indoors and requires a dead man's ghost as an intermediary for the summoning of Sibylia. A second spell calls upon three sisters Milia, Achilia and Sibylia to provide the magician with a ring of invisibility. It is Sibylia who is the focus of attention and, as in the spell published by Katherine Briggs that is referred to at the end of the chapter on folktale fairy and magician stuff, the other two fairies are passed over for Sibylia.

In another ritual seven sisters including Delforia, are summoned in the name of 'Inferiours & servants to the Emprice & princes of all fayres Sibilis.'[11]

Somehow Llyfr Cyfrin has joined Sibylia to the seven sisters. This may have occurred before the Welsh adaptation, but as Ellis Edwart/Dafydd Dafis has 'Ilia', it seems possible that it was the compiler of Llyfr Cyfrin who did it. Perhaps 'Ilia' suggested 'Sibyllia' and thus

'Sibi'.

Sibli was the word in Welsh for Sibyl, the female oracles from the classical world who were perpetuated in Christian tradition as their prophecies were construed to have predicted Christianity. The Sibyl was known in medieval welsh tradition as is shown by *Dared Phrygia*, a popular medieval version of the Tale of Troy, and from a triad, one of the mnemonic devices that acted as a kind of index for Welsh lore, that refers to Sibli Doeth, Sibli the Wise.[12]

Thus the substitution of Sibli for Ilia connected the sisters with an entirely different strand of Welsh tradition.In later Welsh sources Sibyl came to be a generic term for an enchantress.

While it seems very unlikely that names from the seven sisters spell spread out into the Welsh folk tradition, the reverse may well be true. The Llyfr Cyfrin version is unique in referring to the sister as Sibia. In both the Llyfr Dewiniaeth and Testunau Swyngyfaredd versions the name is Lilia, as it is in Sloane MS 3824. Thus it may be the case that the dyn hysbys of Llyfr Cyfrin substituted Sibia for Lilia based on his knowledge of the Braich-y-Dinas story or some other story involving Sibia.

The very same spell was also found in another cunning man's notebook from around the same time. This was the notebook of Dafydd Dafis (Dauydd Dauis) which survives in a copy made by one Edward Ellis. Ellis' copy is in the National Library of Wales at Aberystwyth but has never been transcribed. 13

However, J. H. Davies. who used the pen-name Penardd wrote an article on Edwart Ellis in 1901 in the series Lloffion Llenyddol for a London-based Welsh-language newspaper titled the *London Kelt* or *Kelt Llundain*. Penardd lists several charms and other material from the notebook and gives an extract from the spell. It is clearly of the same origin as the seven sisters spell found in Llyfr Cyfrin but it is a somewhat different and more complete, at least than the spell as given by Kate Bosse-Griffiths.

A further manuscript containing the text is the nineteenth century 'Testunau swyngyfaredd,' NLW 663B. This damaged MS contains 'Hyfforddiad i alw rhyw ffath ar Ysprydion y rhai ai geilw nhw yn Dylwyth Teg' .

These two versions of the spell also closely resemble one in Sloane 3824, given the title *The Book of Treasure Spirits* by David Rankine. This is in English, and in a particularly verbose form of English at that. Much of the material that immediately follows the seven sisters spell is also found in Llyfr Dewiniaeth and in Testunau Swyngyfaredd and Llyfr Cyfrin, proving a close relationship.

In this seven sisters spell in Llyfr Cyfrin we have a quite condensed ritual that draws on a wealth of European tradition and existed in a small notebook written by a Welsh dyn hysbys in the early nineteenth century. Yet Llyfr Cyfrin was only part of the spell's tradition in Wales. Someone–perhaps Dafydd Dafis–had translated it from an English that was already old. Edwart Ellis made his copy from Elis Edwart's version. Our dyn hysbys made his version, perhaps from the same source or an associated one. Testunau Swyngyfaredd also included a slightly variant edition. Then it was published in the London Kelt by Penardd in 1901, collected into his book *Rhai o Hen Ddewiniaid*, and published by Kate Bosse-Griffiths in the 1970s, then included by Angelike Rüdiger in her dissertation. And here it is again, in the twenty-first century, in Wales, once again available to a wider audience.

The Seven Sisters Spell in Sloane MS 3824

There are also another sort of terrestriall spirits of the nature of these next fore spoken of, that Dwell on the Superficies of the Earth, & in the Caves & Caverns thereof, who Likewise haunteth houses and other places, & have the Keeping of Treasures, that are hidden or Buryt therein, who are somewhat more humane & courteous by nature than the former, and are more feminine And delight in the Company of women & Children, and more Especially of Such who are wholly inclined to housewifery, as maidservants &c: but they poor souls being by fear and ignorance also, many times affrighted & astonished, at the Least unusuall Sight or Noyse, of any of them, Do thereby Lose many Benefits Yet not withstanding to such as they bear Love & Kindness too, they are very benevolent and friendly &c: and are again as obnoxious and offensive to them as they hate, And they are a vespertine Nocturnall wandering spirits, who many times will so come to some, even from Sun Setting to its Rising the next morn:-

These Kind of spirits are more frequently visible than any others, and are the Least of the Hierarchies, and where they Haunt or do Keep any hidden Treasures, they make no great matter of Noyse or Disturbance; their Noyse Seemeth much as the treadings & trampling of many people, & sometimes as if there were a preparation to some great feast, as if there were two or three Cooks at work in the Kitching, and the jack going, the Bread Rouling to & fro in the Oven, and all such Kind of Noyses, as if many folks were all at worke, which are not so hideous or terrible as other spirits Do make.-------------

These spirits may be also called upon as the other, in such places where either they haunt or foremost frequent in, and the place which is appointed or set apart for action must be Suffumigated with good Aromatick Odours, and a Cleane Cloath spread on the Ground or a table nine foot Distant from the Circle, upon which there must be Either a Chicken or any Kind of small joynt, or piece of meat handsomely Rosted, and a white mantle, a Basin or little Dish like a Coffe Dish of fair Running water, half a pint of Sack in a botle, a bottle of Ale Containing a Quart, Some food and a pint of Cream in a Dish provided Ceremonies they are much pleased & delighted with; and doth allure them to friendly familiarity willingly & Readyly fullfilling your desires &c: without much Difficulty, and some have used no Circle at all to the Calling of these spirits, but only being Cleane was had and apparelld, sit at another table or place onely Covored with Clean Linnen Cloth, nine foot Distant & so invocate.------------------------

Those Kind of Terrestrial spirits are vulgarly Called of all people generally Fairies or Elphs, and the natures and Quality of them are well Known to many, those spirits there are too who are Set over the Hierarchy as the Supreme head thereof, whose names are Mycob and Oberion, under whome again are Seven Sisters, placed as the next principal, whose names, Are, Lilia, Rostilia, Foca, FolIa, Africa, Julia, Venulla, under whom again are many Legions as Subjects and Subservient &c: who (as aforesaid) wander to & fro upon the Earth, and have the Keeping also of many Treasures that are hidden or Buryed, especially such as are hidden in those places that they frequent, inhabit, or Delight in, and that Are innocently hidden by good honest people;

Either for Security, or future preservation, who many times Dye, & leave it so unrevealed, then are Such treasures Seized on and Kept by these terrestriall Elphs; if ever they happen to come where it is &c: then the Magicall Philosopher understanding, that any treasures are Kept by the terrestriall spirits of this order, And would obtain the Same, and would have converse with them, let him observe the foregoing Directions, and at the appoynted time repair to the place designated for action, and invocate as followeth, I Exorcize, adjure, call upon, urge and Earnestly Require you terrestriall spirits, that are the supreme head of the Hierarchy, of those that Are called Fairies, and who are Called by the names of Mycob and Oberyon, In the name of the Almighty, Everliving and heavenly God Jehova, and of his only Begotten & wellbeloved son Jesus Christ our Lord, Messias, Sother, Emanuel, the high King & Lord of all the world, I do hereby call upon and importinnately Desiring Spirits Mycob and Oberyon, to command the Seven Sisters Lilia, Rostilia, Foca, Folla, Africa, Julia, Venulla, or some one of them, to appear visibly to us, or in Your friendly Benevolence, to send some one or other spirit or spirits, of your Hierarchy or odors, to accommodate instruct and assist us, in such of our Requests wherein they may: The which I confidently & Earnestly importune of you as are our friends, & we are your friends, and all of us servants to the Highest in whose name I now Call upon you and humbly urge, and most Earnestly Desire you, to Send one of the Seven Sisters next subservient under you, to Appear visibly to us, & to assist us in the obtaining and recovering of their Treasures, that are hidden or Buryed in the House or place, or Elsewhere adjacent hereabouts, or to send some one Subject Subservient of your Hierarchy, to Assist and help us herein, and allso in all Such matters And things as we shall Desire their Instructions and accommodations in, xxxx Wherein, they may Continue this invocation for seven nights from the Hour of Eleven till two, and invocate nine times an hour but withall observing that if Any Apparition or Vision should appear, in forme and manner, willing to Commune with us, in the Interim, you may then cease, and desire to Know the name & seal of Such Spirit, and when you have taken a note thereof you may proceed to your Demands, which you ought to have fairly written Down, because then they are In A greater Readiness, and Chargeth not the memory to recollect It Self, for being So stumbled & hobbled in your conceptions, you may Chance to lose that opportunity and peradventure your Design too, but If nothing happens in the interim, then after the first seven nights, always beginning the next night after the Change of the moon, you shall invocate or call upon the Seven Sisters as followeth,

    Sator Arepo Tenet Opera Rotas
Kyrie Eloyson. Christe Eloyson. Kyrie Eloyson.
Adonay Cui Pater Cui Filius
    Cui Spiritus Sanctus Allelujah.

I exorcise, adjure command constrain &, most Earnestly urge and request you Akorayes, the Sisters of those terrestriall spirits, who are Called Fairies or Elphs by & in the name of the incomprehensable God of heaven &, Earth, &, all Creatures whatsoever are there In Contained and Comprehended, Jehovah, Elohim, Agla, El, Tetragrammaton, &, in the name of Jesus Christ, begotten of a Virgin by the Holy Ghost, and born in the flesh at Nazareth, the second person In tninity, And the Saviour of the World.

Especially of all believers, &, those who lay hold upon him by faith, Thereby Confidently and finnly laying hold on the promises, that whatsoever we Ask our Heavenly Father, or shall any ways act, or do in his name, nothing shall be Denied us, nor be impossible to us, in whose name & through whose authority we as true believers do Call upon, constraine and very Confidently Urgently and Earnestly Importune you, in the name also, and by the power of the Head and Supreme of your orders, or Hierarchy, and to whom you are the next In Order, governing over many Legions of other your Subjects & Subservients or some one of you Lilia, Rostilia, Foca, Folla, Africa, Julia, Venulla, to appear visibly to us, or to send someone other of your Subjected Subservients to help and Assist us in the obtaining of the treasures that are hidden or Buryed in this house or place, or Elsewhere adjacent hereabouts, And more Especially the spirit or spirits that hath the Keeping thereof, Leave, Be Discharged & quit therefrom, & so avoid the same, and forthwith to Donate,

Yield up & Surrender the Same, into our possession, so that we may bear the same away, and convert it to our necessary uses, without fraud or any other Crafts or Subtilltyes, that may in any wise deprive us thereof, I do once again Exorcize, adjure and command thee Lilia & all thy Sisters & subjects By the imperiall throne, and by the majesty & Deity of the Everliving God, that some or other spirit of your orders, and more Especially Such spirit or spirits, that have the Keeping of the treasures that are Hidden or Buryed In this house or place, or near adjacent hereabouts Do appear visibly before us, to Resolve us friendly, and verily in all such Matters & things, as we shall rationally Desire, and Demand of you, that Amongst the Rest in partickular as concerning our recovering and obtaining the treasures, that Lyeth hidden or Buryed here or Elsewhere, let the spirit or spirits that hath the Keeping thereof, be Discharged and quitted of It, & immediately in all peace & quietness avoid & Depart therefrom, and Permit & yeald up the Same to us as aforesaid: And the Peace of God always Remaine Betweene you & us, in the name of the Father & of the Son and of the holy Ghost, And do for us herein as for the servants of the highest, Let the first of these four invocations be observed to be practiced, the first seven nights of the moons encrease, Beginning the next night after She Change, as is before taught, and then the Eighth night, beginneth the Latter, & invocate nine times an hour, in the right season, from Eleven of the Clock till two, for that they being most frequently then visible, and stirring about, therefore Most convenient, and opportune, to Call upon them: for God hath So decreed, that they Shall not be visible and frequent in the Day as in the night, Except they are privately Called upon in the Day, because they shall not be frightfull nor offensive, to harmless & innocent people, for he hath bounded all things, and they Cannot pass their Limits without permission.----------

The Seven Sisters Spell 139

This Circle And Pentacle Serveth to all the whole foregoing Experiment

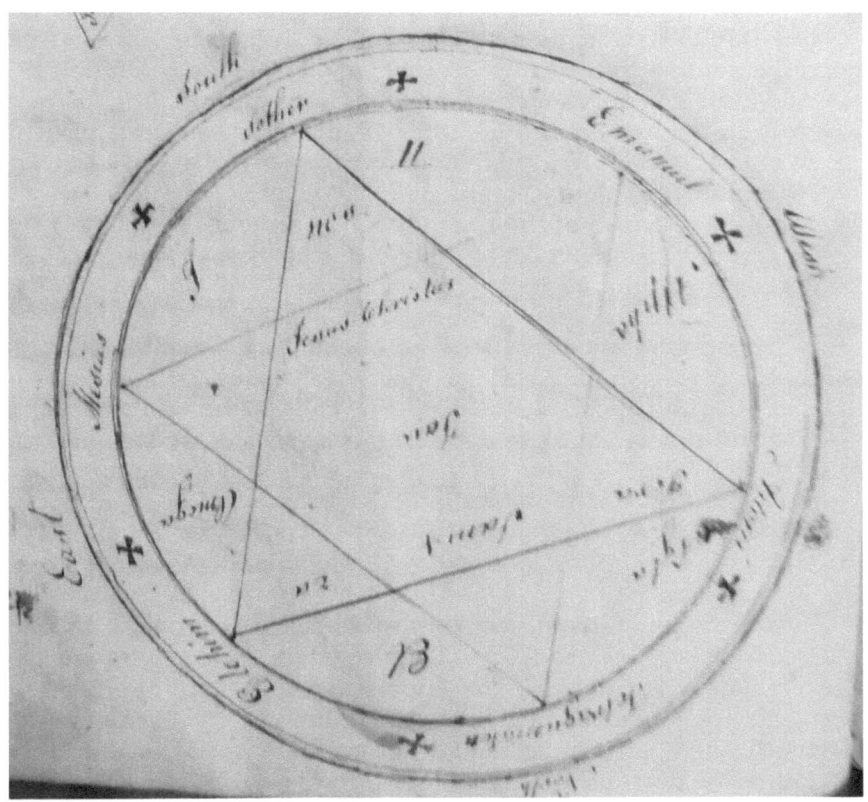

This copy of the circle is taken from the seven sisters spell in Testunau Swyngyfaredd, NLW 663B.

Notes

1 *The Fourth Book of Occult Philosophy* p.55.
2 See Daniel Harms, 'Hell and Fairy: The Differentiation of Fairies and Demons Within British Ritual Magic of the Early Modern Period,' in *Knowing Demons, Knowing Spirits in the Early Modern Period*, edited by Michelle D. Brock, Richard Raiswell, and David R. Winter, 2018, Palgrave Macmillan,]
3 Harms in *The Faerie Queens* (p. 59). Avalonia.
4 A full comparison of the Llyfr Cyfrin seven spirits spell and o=the other versions is beyond the scope of this volume but I hope to return to it in another book.
5 Harms in *The Faerie Queens* (p. 59). Avalonia. In the Ellis Edwart version they are referenced once only as Micopau and Oberian. Micob's name varies considerably in traditions outside Llyfr Cyfrin–as Micob/Micol/Mical/Mycob. Micob and Oberian (as Toberian because someone has mistaken a cross between the two names for a 'T') along with the SATOR square (also mispelt) are used for a paper talisman to catch thieves in Robert Roberts' *Seryddiaeth.*
6 Harms in *The Faerie Queens* (p. 59). Avalonia.
7 'Seven evil sisters were identified as the chills and fevers [Olsan: 'In a late fifteenth century manuscript in a charm labelled "a good prayer," we read, . . . I conjure (coniuro) you who are seven sisters, the first Daliola, the second Vestulia, the third Fugalia, the fourth Suferalie, the fifth Affrecta, the sixth Lilia, the seventh Luctalia through the Father and Son and Holy Spirit and through the day of days and through the mercy of our Lord Jesus Christ and through all the angels, archangels and through the apostles, martyrs, confessors and virgins and all the saints of God though all the powers of heaven and earth and sea and all that are in them . . .
Their names vary. In another, longer, more carefully written version of the charm from the fifteenth century, they are conjured as Ylya, Saytulia, Viole, Sursoralia, Seneya, Deneya, and Emyra in that order one to seven. Writing On The Hand in Ink: A Late Medieval Innovation in Fever Charms in England, Lea T. Olsan]
8 Harms 'Hell and Fairy' p. 66-67.
9 Bosse-Griffiths writes
Some of these names sound strangely familiar.
Bychan ŵyr fy meistres i

Mai Jili Ffrwtan ydwy i (30, t. 102)
Little knows my mistress
That I am Jili Ffrwtan

Yn Llŷn fe genid y geiriau hyn yn dawel, wrth nyddu, gan un o'r Tylwyth Teg a oedd mewn gwasanaeth gyda phobl feidrol. Tybed ai Julia'r ysbryd oedd hon. Affrit yw'r gair Arabeg am ysbryd. Ai Julia'r ysbryd oedd hi felly?
Gwyddys hefyd am Sibi. un arall o'r Tylwyth Teg, a addawodd briodi llanc o Fraich-y-Ddinas ar yr amod y llwyddai i ddarganfod beth oedd ei henw (37a). Onid yr un oedd hon â Sibia, neu Sibi, un o'r saith chwaer?
In Llŷn these words were sung quietly, while [banking a fire?], by one of the Tylwyth Teg who was in service with powerful/mighty people. I wonder whether Julia was this spirit. Affrit is the Arabic word for a spirit. So was Julia this spirit?
Sibi is also known, another of the Tylwyth Teg, who promised to marry a lad of Braich-y-Ddinas on the condition that he was successful in discovering what was her name. Was she not the same as Sibia, or Sibi, one of the Seven Sisters?
Rudiger responds:
> This evidence does not support the hypothesis that 'sili ffrit' was based on the charm with the names of the seven sisters. In absence of further evidence, it could be that the similarity in sound of 'sili ffit' and Affrita is simply accidental. In connection with changeling tales, 'sili ffrit', 'silly good-for-nothing person', would make sense. 'Sibia' or 'Sibi' could be a truncated form of Sibylla (Lat.) or Sibile (Old French), both without relating to the charm. Harms draws attention to the fact that the Sibyls of the Classical became reinterpreted as fairy characters in the Middle Ages (2018, p. 63). Therefore, a form of Sibyl appearing in folk tradition as fairy name must not necessarily been connected to the charm. We must note that Sibia appears in the Welsh charm which presents the youngest version of the seven sisters who are interpreted as Tylwyth Teg in that charm. We could therefore assume that the redactor of the charm has replaced a version of 'Ilia' by a typical fairy name. Furthermore, Bosse-Griffiths suggests that 'Folla' could be derived from the Irish triad of 'Folla, Banba, Éire' (Bosse-Griffiths, 1977, p. 126). But as the older charms relating to the seven sisters were popular in Scandinavia and Germany, an Irish origin is not as likely as changes due to consecutive scribal variations.

10 Rhŷs *Celtic Folklore* p.99-97.
11 Harms *The Faerie Queens* (p. 63).

12 Triad 49. Three People who received the Wisdom of Adam:
Cato the Old,
and Bede,
and Sibli the Wise.
They were, all three, as wise as Adam himself.
Rachel Bromwich, *Trioedd Ynys Prydein: The Triads of the Island of Britain* 4th edition (University of Wales Press, 2017) p. 499.
13 Two photographs of pages of the notebook are included in Lisa Tallis' *Cas Gan Cythraul.* (T. P., (Lisa Tallis, ed.) *Cas Gan Gythraul: Demonology, Witchcraft, and Popular Magic in Eighteenth-Century Wales.* South Wales Record Society, 2015.) It also seems likely that the notebook was used as a source for Robert Roberts' *Seryddiaeth.*]

Bela Fawr by Edward Pugh from *Cambria Depicta* (1816).

Magic in Denbighshire

Denbighshire is a part of Wales with a particularly rich tradition of magic, extending from literary accounts of female and male magicians and fortune-tellers–Gwen ferch Ellis, Huw Lloyd and the witches, Bela Fawr, Sioned Gorn, Sydney, Miss Lloyd Lôn y Parc, John Evans Ffynnon Elian–to court records, folklore and folktales and archaeological finds. Denbighshire has existed as a county in every-shifting forms in North East Wales since the sixteenth century apart from a 22 year period when it was subsumed into the large county of Clwyd. Contemporary Denbighshire is a local authority which has different boundaries to the historical county. Its geography ranges from rolling hillforted hills to heather moors, beautiful lakes and valleys and the most extensive heavy industry in Wales outside of Glamorgan and Gwent.

While I have retained Kate Bosse-Griffiths' naming of the notebook as that of the cunning man of Denbighshire, the only evidence that the Llyfr Cyfrin is from Denbighshire is the author's English-language journal note in which he meets in Wrexham with a farmer from the village of Hope in Flintshire, around five miles from Wrexham in the south east corner of Denbighshire. This is indisputable evidence that the dyn hysbys of

Llyfr Cyfrin sometimes operated in the general area of Denbighshire. Although Hope is just a few miles away the writer feels he should specify that it is in Flintshire, thus suggesting that Denbighshire is where he lived and practised. On the other hand, he feels the need to mention, in a piece of writing recorded only in his personal notebook, that it was in Wrexham that they met, alternatively suggesting that this was out of the usual run of things.[1]

Our sources of information on the magical tradition in Denbighshire come from court records, folklore collections and literary travel writing. There were a few prosecutions for witchcraft in Wales, which along with court cases concerned with the slander of calling someone a witch, give us some evidence of the kinds of practice going on in Wales. There was no witchhunting craze in Wales. Only eight people were successfully prosecuted for witchcraft in Wales, five of whom were executed by hanging, a remarkably low figure. These cases were all in the sixteenth and seventeenth centuries.

Some legends took place in or near Denbighshire. The preacher, poet and reputed reputed magician Huw Llwyd (1568-1630) encountered witches transformed into cats when he stayed in a house on an old road between Cerrig-y-drudion and Betws-y-Coed. The witch Beti'r Baden ('Betty of the wooden frame') used to live up a tree called Pren Gwyn (White Tree) on the crossroads between Conwy and Betws y Coed near Llanrwst in the late sixteenth century. John Wynn of Gwydir had a man spying for him who told him that Beti was a witch and Sir John took his men with him to form a circle around the tree with candles to burn her down. When she was forced down from the tree she went onto her knees to curse him but he told her to leave the area lest she be burned to death.[2]

Gwen ferch Ellis has become the most famous of the historical witches. Executed in 1594 (hanging was the method of killing witches in England and Wales) for murder by witchcraft, hers was was the first definite trial for harmful witchcraft in Wales.

Born about 1552 in Llandyrnog in the Vale of Clwyd, Gwen was twice widowed and three times married. She made treatments for sick animals and also used healing charms for humans. A long charm was recited by Gwen was recorded in court. Containing potentially ancient features it is a unique and valuable example of an older style of charm. When a different charm that was written backwards was found at the house of Justice of the Peace Thomas Mostyn Gwen was accused of having cursed him as the charm was written backwards. When her house was searched a tin or brass image of Christ and a clapperless bell were found, items which could have had a witchcraft function or were at least indicative of residual Catholic sympathies in newly protestant Wales. Hostile witnesses accused Gwen of a variety of malefic magical acts. These ranged from making insane a man who had struck her to having a fly the size of a bumblebee as her familiar. (The fly had been on top of drinks that a group of men had forced Gwen to served to them.) She was the first woman to be hanged for witchcraft in Wales. It seems that her misfortune was partly a function of class, of being accused by a wealthy man.

Later court cases typically focused on fraud rather than witchcraft. The case of Ann Jones or Elen Gilbert in 1635 who conned clients into loaning money for fairies which was never returned was discussed in the chapter on the links between fairies and magicians.

Disappointed clients sometimes sued practitioners. Conjuring–the summoning of spirits–was considered to be rather more pernicious than divination was. The number of court cases must have been tiny in comparison with the number of people who used magical services so we must suppose that either clients were more or less happy with the results or they lacked the means to pursue legal action or had some other reason not to make a public accusation.

Robert Darcy was a Wrexham cunning man and tailor who denied being a conjuror but told fortunes. He could, he said, tell the identity of thieves by the planets, for which claim he was indicted unsuccessfully in 1740 for defrauding one Edward Phillips (who wished to know who had stolen his yarn) of sixpence.[3] Darcy said that if he could not detect the thief successfully the failure 'would make him uneasy in his mind and trouble him for three months afterwards.' Darcy told fortunes by playing cards, shuffling the deck three times before reading the spread of cards.

Apart from literary accounts, court records, written spells and folklore, the material remains of archeology provides one more source of evidence. I know of no charms that have been found in Denbighshire, but a recent modern discovery in Denbigh illustrates the kind of anti-witchcraft artefacts that survive.

In 2020 Lecturer Kerrie Jackson and her husband Bleddyn, to whose family the house had belonged for centuries, discovered beneath a staircase a horde of protective objects. The most mundane of these were a wool hat, shoes of various kinds, from workmen's boots to toddlers' bootees, and parts of a gun barrel and fragments of a horse's skull. Shoes were often positioned in significant places, such as chimneys or stairwells. Their exact purpose is unknown but they are thought to have been intended to ward off evil spirits.[4]

Three women of Denbigh, the titular town in the north west of the county, were well known in the eighteenth and early nineteenth centuries for divination and other magical services: Sioned (Sionnett) Gorn, Old Sydney (Sudna) and Bela (Rebela) Fawr. They had notable successors.

There were also celebrated witches at Denbigh. Bela Fawr (Big Bella) was one of the last and most famous of her tribe in that town, and many other places were credited with possessing persons endowed with witching powers, as well as those who could break spells.[5]

They must have made a considerable impact on inhabitants of Denbighshire as their reputations have survived in a wide variety of forms.

Bela was credited with a very successful unwitching of cattle in Llanfrothen in 1815. (See the chapter on bewitched cattle for the full text of this.)

The later reputation of these three derives partly from a mention in *Pleser a Gof*, a 1787 dramatic comedy which was one of the interludes of Twm o'r Nant ('Tom of the Brook', Thomas Edwards.) These were verse dramas, mostly humorous, and written using the complex traditional Welsh metres. Occasional pieces of dialogue were in English. These were also in cynghanedd, the elaborate system of sound correspondences that is unique to the welsh language and adapted to the language over centuries. The English sections combine a tour de force of technique with comic effect.

A character named Rondol has his fortune told by an 80 year old Gypsy woman named Sali o'r Sowth (Sally of the south), for which she requests a piece of bacon (batch) as long as her arm and as much grain. Rondol is so pleased with the consultation that he exclaims (in English) 'Sian and Sioned, and Rebela of Dinbych, They're not fit to open their mouth'[6] Rebela of Dinbych is Bella fawr, Sioned is Sioned Gorn. Twm o'r Nant's Sian is less easy to identify: it was Hen Sidney, Old Sidney who usually completed the magical triumverate with Sioned and Bela.

It was Edward Pugh, an artist and author of *Cambria Depicta*, who mentions Sioned Gorn and met Bela Fawr, whose portrait he drew.

Sioned's epithet, Gorn (Welsh Corn from the Latin cornu) refers to her distinctive ornamentation.

Y Sioned, y ddewines arall a nodir gan Twm, a adwaenid yn well fel Sioned Gorn, am y byddai'n gwisgo corn gafr wrth linyn am ei gwddf. Ond, fel llawer crefft enillfawr arall yn man drefydd Cymru, rhaid rhestru dewiniaeth hefyd bellach yn mysg eu 'lapsed industries.'[7]

Sioned, the other dewines noted by Twm, was known best as Sioned Gorn, for she wore a goat's horn on a string around her neck. But like many other lucrative crafts in the towns of Wales, witchcraft must be listed among the 'lapsed industries.'

The horn is an instance of the tendency of cunning folk in Wales to adopt extravagant dress. The Devil's Bum Naili from Llanrhaedr-ym-Mochnant in Montgomeryshire is the most notable example, wearing a high-crowned sheepskin cap with a plume of pigeon's feathers, a robe covered with magical symbols and a wand with a bone handle and eel-skin thong. Others wore clothing adorned with magical and astrological symbols. Hen Jem once wore purple silk robes to a Breconshire court.[8]

Edward Pugh made a portrait of Bela, reproduced at the beginning of this chapter, depicting her as a respectably dressed and demure woman with none of the outrageous attire just mentioned but with a pack of playing cards and two small books.

His description of his encounter with her in his *Cambria Depicta* is worth reproducing in full:

Here lived, a few years ago, a fortune-teller, of the name of Sionett Gorn. On her death, it was not likely that so lucrative an office should be suffered to lie dormant; and it has, ever since, been filled up by two wonderful women; of whom it is reported that they can see into futurity with half an eye, and that many of their remarkable predictions have been eventually verified. Among their devotees I had the curiosity to pay a visit to the one most in repute. I was requested to take a seat in the passage, the lady being then deeply engaged in her calculations on the fate of a man, who was weak enough, as I understood, to come from Barmouth, a distance of sixty miles, to consult this old woman. I could plainly hear their conversation. It seems that this person had a complaint upon him, similar to a consumption; which was not understood by the faculty of the neighbourhood; but which he fancied to have been the effect of a curse, on a visit to Llanelian well, by some secret enemy. She managed this man's case with a good deal of art, and, it may be added, with–excellent advice. She told him that he might easily prevent any mischief to himself, by frequent petitions to the Almighty; and that he might rest assured if he did not succeed, that the fault was his own, in not praying with that degree of fervency which his case required: but that if he should prove sincere, he would get the better of his complaint in a short time. After paying the fee, he was dismissed, and I was ushered into the presence of this awful divineress. I was requested to take a chair opposite to hers, when she wished I would tell her the business I came upon, and be free and communicative. I took out my sketchbook: but being dilatory in my reply, 'Come, come,' said she, 'I know your concerns, you are bashful, a thing very common to those who apply to me: but, as there are only you and I in the room, you need not be under the least apprehension of being heard. But,' continued she, 'I know your business and employment: you are a merchant, and are travelling among your correspondents in this country: but you have been somewhat unhappy for some time, and (with a smile and a bending of the head) you are in love with a pretty lady, whom at present you cannot obtain; but be not too much cast down, the lady is yours.' Upon this I replied, that she had well predicted my case:- that I had, accordingly, partly secured the lady already; but wished to know if she liked her, at the same time shewing her her own portrait, in sketching which I had been tolerably successful. She appeared very angry; and whatever use I intended to make of it, she said, she cared very little; she was conscious of having done no harm to any one. The proffered fee, however, appeased her resentment, and we parted very good friends.

The money this woman gets in this way, enables her and her sprightly daughter to live and dress well; and her respectable appearance only increases her consequence among the deluded, who are eager to listen to her jargon nonsense. As since the union of Wales with England, our laws are one and the same, it is pity that these impostors should be allowed thus to cheat the deluded poor! Our magistrates, no doubt, are just as capable of preventing their depredations on the hard earnings of the 'labourer, as those of London were, in putting an end to the imposture of Mrs. Williams.[9]

The activities of Elen Ann Pughe were more restricted.

Elen did not claim to be able to handle spirits. Her path was more concerned with the world of romance. At night she was able to do her work. Many of the single class approached her, men and women, to try to find out each other's history from her. She claimed to be able to interpret some mysteries in the business of love, and it is very easy in every age to find customers who have a deep desire to know each other's history. Nel's sun went down like Bela's, and they were replaced by a brighter sun in the person of one named Miss Lloyd.

She was a strange creature, seeming to have been in continual communion with unearthly beings. In the kitchen she had a squirrel, and a guinea-pig running around. When someone came to the house, these creatures entertained themselves, by making the loudest noise, to reassure customers that their mistress was having contact with someone who was helping her in the art.[10]

Her life had its complexities. She was known as 'Miss' Lloyd but had a son named Edwin, presumably as a result of the following incident: 'She fell in love with a young gentleman, and the love affair went on for some time. But when he was about to go and marry her, the young man's wife came into sight, and the young man ran away, and was never seen again.'

The account in 'Dewinesau Dinbych', included in the appendices, gives several instances of successful examples of divination and finding lost objects.

Her end was a sad one.

> ... one night she went to Edwin Hughes' vaults to ask for a shilling of liquor, and she said to the barman,—'I never had such a job to come up the alley as tonight.' 'What's the matter, Miss Lloyd?' he said. 'Well,' she said, 'they were around me like bees tonight; I would for the life of me ignore them.' Having got the liqueur, she went home talking loudly to herself the whole way. She died at the bottom of Henllan Street at a considerable age, and is said to have looked awful at the end of her life.

Depending on the paradigm used, Miss Lloyd was either plagued by spirits that she was unable to keep under control or suffered from some mental illness.

Old Sydney was another eccentric who was accused of deception.

> In one of those little thatched cabins standing on the brink of this pool, once lived that notorious imposter 'Old Sydney,' one of the three celebrated Denbigh Witches: Bella, Sydney, and Sioned Gorn, who carried on a most lucrative business, by imposing upon the credulity of the superstitious and evil-minded portion of the community, pretending to foretell future events, discover lost or stolen property, and restore quiet to haunted mansions and localities frequented by evil spirits, and were frequently employed, (like Balaam of old,) by malicious people, to cure and bewitch their enemies. Their employees and accomplices acted in the character of ghosts, and 'played the devil,' whenever occasion required. The reader will not demand a voucher for the truth of the following anecdote, further than that it has long passed current as a fact: One night, three young men called upon Old Sydney for their 'fortunes,' when one of them, who was considered more daring than the rest, expressed a particular desire to see the devil, and offered a handsome fee if she

could gratify his curiosity; to which she replied, that she was quite capable of exhibiting the evil one, but thought he had not the nerve to look Satan in the face. He, however, assured her that he had; but doubted whether she was sufficiently initiated into the mysteries of the black art to 'call up spirits from the vasty deep.' At last, tempted by the proffered fee, and wishing to remove the reflection cast upon her necromancing powers, she consented to introduce his demonship into the presence of the trio, two of whom had already began to feel a little nervous palpitation about the heart. Having cautioned them not to move or speak, she went through some mysterious mummeries, and blew out the candle; when suddenly the rattle of chains, accompanied by unearthly noises, were heard to issue from the adjoining chamber, the door of which was gently drawn aside. The dim light of the embers smouldering on the cabin hearth, just afforded them a misty sight of the spirit of darkness, now metamorphosed into an ox, butting the door with his horns, and stamping the threshold with his hoofs, his eyes glistening with phosphoric vividness, and then withdrawing. Two of the spectators were terror-stricken, but our hero shouted 'Come forward, Satan, don't be afraid to show yourself.' The demon made a rush forward, with a fiendish bray. At that instant, a large mastiff which our wag had brought along with him, and which, until then, lay couching quietly at his feet, imagining that the devil growled at him, and wished to 'show fight,' sprang at the apparition, caught Satan by the throat, threw him prostrate on the floor, and would have worried him, there and then, had he not screamed out 'murder!' Our hero quickly ran to his aid, and having released him from his canine antagonist, and stripped him of the bullock's hide in which he was habited, there at once recognised this demon to be a well-known accomplice of our witch, whom she had charitably fostered and reared from an imp, and who had been for many years a ghost, and had, moreover, been publicly whipped through a certain market town as an incorrigible thief. The sequel need not be told, further than that, in some oral versions of the tale, it is added, he never recovered of the injuries inflicted upon him by the dog. Our second-sighted ladies had a short and ready method with troublesome ghosts and sprights, whom they confined, for periods differing from a few years to ten or twenty centuries, between the bark and timber of a growing tree, between two bricks in a chimney, under a large stone, or such like secure place. But it not unfrequently happened, in felling a tree, or taking down an old building, that some ghost of 'olden time' broke loose, and became doubly furious and terrible, in which case, the owners or occupiers of such property were put to the expense of transporting the demon to the Red Sea. Thanks to the spread of Scriptural knowledge, education, and general intelligence, those superstitious notions, current even in our own youthful days, have now almost become matters of history; although the race of witches and fortune-tellers is not yet quite extinct in this part of the world.[11]

In an appendix I include 'Dewinesau Dinbych', 'The Witches of Denbigh', in full. The translation is mine and it is the first time it has appeared in English.

By far the most famous magical site in north Wales during the eighteenth and nineteenth centuries was Ffynnon Elian, the Well of St Elian. Wales abounded with healing wells which were dedicated to local saints. Some were utilised mostly by local people, some specialised in specific ailments such as eye disorders, some were famous far beyond their parishes. The founding legend of Ffynnon Elian as a holy well involved a hermit saint who fell ill and prayed for water. Water appeared at his side and he was cured upon drinking from it, a miracle of a sort that also inaugurated other healing wells in Wales. By the late eighteenth century it had become a well for cursing, not healing. Suggett devoted several pages to Ffynon Elian. Jane Beckerman, the current owner of the property on which the well is situated, has written a short informative book on the history of Ffynon Elian, Unholy Water. There is so much information on the well that even this is not exhaustive.

The well became both popular and notorious. Many people seem to have come to the well in the sincere belief that the well would help them right wrongs and reverse injustices. Many commentators have pointed out that life was hard for many people at the time during which Ffynnon Elian thrived. The common land that had traditionally been used for grazing was being whittled away by acts of enclosure, the weather was bad and crops were poor, corn prices were high and stable though poor ways of life were rapidly eroded by industrialisation and new crops. No wonder that aggrieved people who were victims of injustice or who felt they had been wronged by equally poor neighbours look to cursing wells for some small advantage in their difficult lives.

The curse involved placing a piece of slate or lead or a pebble into the well with the victim's initials on it. Some sort of ritual was usually enacted and the keeper of the well charged a fee. The profitable nature of the well quickly turned it into a scam. Not only were people being charged to place someone into the well, perceived victims of a Ffynnon Elian curse had to pay for their names to be removed from the well, whether they were actually 'in the well' or not. This form of magic, in which service magicians are paid to curse, counter-curse and lift curses comes to resemble the legal profession in which lawsuits are met with countersuits and dismissals. In the latter it is only the lawyers who win, in the former it is only the magicians who win.

There were allegations that slates, stones and pebbles inscribed with pairs of initials were placed into the well in advance ready to be removed from the well as the curse was lifted, even if no curse had been placed in the first place. In nineteenth century Wales most people had anglicized names and surnames were famously limited. Thus there were John Roberts and Mary Jones aplenty. An initial like J.E. could account for hundred of Johns, Janes and James who were Edwards, Evans, Eynons and Ellises.

There were several attempts to destroy it or to make the activities illegal. The walls enclosing the well house were destroyed in 1814. In 1819 John Edwards was imprisoned for 12 months for fraud for convincing an Edward Pierce that his name had been put into the well. (See chapter Shon y Rhoses for more on this case.) John Evans took over as keeper of the well by having the water diverted onto his own neighbouring property. In 1826 use of the well was forbidden and the well house was demolished by the local Methodists in 1829. John Evans was finally imprisoned in 1854 having profited from Ffynon Elian for around 35 years. Even after Evans had repented, joined the Baptists and written a memoir about his time as keeper of the well, pinned corks were being put into the well.[12]

When Pugh wrote his account of Bela Fawr in *Cambria Depicta* he mentioned that her previous customer, who was receiving a consultation while Pugh waited, was from Barmouth and believed he was cursed and his name had perhaps been put into the well at Llanelian.

The well has been restored by the current owner of the property.

Ffynnon Elian maintained its notoriety long after it ceased to function either as a holy well or a cursing well. One conduit of its persistence in popular memory is the following short tale from *The Welsh Fairy Book* by William Jenkyn.

PEDWS FFOWK AND ST ELIAN'S WELL

Pedws Ffowk was for three years afflicted with a complaint which nobody could understand. She was well and yet she was not well: she was sick and yet she was not sick. That is to say, she had no ache or pain, and her appetite was good. But all the time she became thinner and thinner, until at last she was nothing but skin and bone. She went to doctor after doctor, but they could not find out what was the matter with her. She consulted quacks also, but even they did her no good. Finally, she went to a wise man. He, after hearing her story, said, 'Someone has put you into St. Elian's Well.'

'What do you mean by that?' asked Pedws.

'Someone has gone to the woman who keeps. the well,' answered the wise man, 'and put your name on the register, and thrown a pin into the well, together with a pebble with your initials on it.'

'Well, what is the harm of that?' inquired Pedws, who had not heard of the power of the cursing well.

'You are cursed,' was the reply, 'and unless the curse is removed, you will pine away and die.'

'But what am I to do?' said Pedws, now thoroughly frightened.

'You must go to the woman who keeps the well, and pay her to take you out of the well,' was the wise man's advice.

Pedws lost no time in going to the guardian of the well, who, for a small fee, agreed to examine her register. Sure enough, the name of Pedws Ffowk was there inscribed, and the date of the entry corresponded with the time when she had begun to waste away. On the payment of another and a larger sum of money the priestess of the fountain agreed to take out of the water the stone on which the initials of Pedws Ffowk were scratched. From that moment flesh began to grow on her bones, and before long her clothes, which had hung upon her like rags upon a scarecrow, were filled out as well as they had ever been. Pedws lived to a good old age, and her greatest trouble was that she never found out which of her best friends had put her into the well.[13]

Mochyn y Nant, also known as the conjuror of Ruabon, was yet another John Roberts. He was remembered in England chiefly through a rather sarcastic piece written by Thomas de Quincey, the English Opium Eater but as an 1806 obituary put it,

Mochyn was conjuror and fortuneteller to a great part of the Principality, and his fame extended far into Shropshire and Cheshire. He professed to have attained his science in Egypt, though he was scarcely ever beyond his parish bounds. He was continually resorted to for the recovery of strayed linen, poultry, hatchets and asses – even his name served to make rogues observe the rules of honesty. When he could not make out infallibly the offender, he still was able to afflict him with any infirmity or disease the injured party did like – ague, rheumatism, and St. Vitus Dance, were entirely at his command, and dealt out by him in the most liberal manner. In fortune telling he no less excelled; no swain or maid ever applied in vain: he could not only create love in the human breast, but also chill it with aversion and disdain. For these purposes he gave, or rather sold, charms couched in dark hieroglyphic characters, which were also in much request to ensure success in any enterprize – a rat race or a cock fight.[14]

His expertise extended to exorcising ghosts:-

Haunted houses, of which report asserts there is one, at least, in every Parish, were soon by his Magic freed from their nocturnal visitors. No Ghost possessed sufficient temerity to withstand his solemn Incantations. In vain the perturbed Spirit pleaded for the privilege of longer wandering thro' her favorite Rooms, or 'visiting the glimpses of the Moon,' the Conjuror was inexorable, and the disappointed Ghost was reluctantly by his command consigned to the bottom of the Red Sea.[15]

Yet there were also memories of ineffective remedies or inaccurate divinations. Jonathan Hughes the bard lampooned Mochyn's advice to one William Williams who had a sheep stolen, which was found strangled some weeks in some loose straw in a building later. Mochyn y Nant gave Williams a piece of paper to put under his head, telling him that he would see the thief in a dream.

The Mochyn promised Williams in a second journey to show the thief's face in a glass, and also to place a mark on his nose,' and then suddenly added, 'You had better go home, and put this paper in the soil of his garden, and the thief will never be at ease.

The implied outcome seems to be that the thief was never identified.

Elias Owen records a chilling tale about an unnamed dyn hysbys.

> There was also a well-known charmer who lived at Llandegla, Denbighshire, who refused a charm to a certain man. When asked why he had not complied with his request, he said – 'He will not need charms for his birds, for he will be a dead man before the main comes off.' This became true, for the man died, as foretold.

Two other dyn hysbys or conjurors who were active in or near Denbighshire will be discussed in further chapters. One of them may conceivably be the author of the Llyfr Cyfrin. The other is mentioned in the notebook itself as an unsuccessful rival.

When the dyn hysbys of the Llyfr Cyfrin met his farmer client in 1832 some skeptics were already saying that the writing was on the wall for the cunning folk of popular renown. In the March 1829 issue of the periodical *Lleuad yr Oes* (The Moon of the age) one contributor known only as preswylydd arall yn Nghaerludd ('another resident of London') proclaimed the end of Welsh superstition.

> Y mae Dic Smot yn y bedd, y plant bychain yn gwybod pethau gwell; Bella yn farw, gwybodaeth yn blodeuo; Ffynon Eilian wedi sychu, gardd addysg yn cael ei dwfrhau...
>
> Dic Smot is in the grave, the little children know better things; Bella is dead, knowledge is in bloom; Ffynon Eilian is dried up, the garden of education is watered...[16]

Yet while their heyday might have been coming to an end, cunning folk still practised in Wales well into the twentieth century. Folklorists and journalists alike reported that cunning folk and conjurors were still active in rural Wales in the 1930s and tales about earlier magicial practitioners were still current.

Mary Lewes recounts a story which makes the legendary magician Robin Ddu active in Denbighshire.

> The following story which I find amongst my notes, well illustrates the kind of affair about which these seers were constantly consulted.
>
> A gentleman in Denbighshire, lost a large silver cup of much value, which had been an heirloom for several generations. After making diligent inquiries respecting the cup without success, he determined to place the affair in the hands of Robin Ddu, the wizard. Robin attended at the hall, and after placing his red cap on his head, he called the inmates of the hall before him, and declared he would find the thief before midnight. All the servants denied the theft. 'Then,' said Robin, 'if you are guiltless, you will have no objection to a magic proof.' He then ordered a cockerel to be placed under a pot in the pantry, and told all the servants to go and rub the pot with both their hands. If any of them were guilty, the cockerel would crow whilst the thief was rubbing the vessel. After all had gone through the ceremony, the wizard ordered them to show their hands, when he perceived that the hands of the butler were clean. His conscience had stricken him so that he could not touch the pot. Robin accused him of the theft, which he admitted, and the cup was restored to its owner.[17]

Yet the traditional cunning folk of Wales are no more.

It didn't last. Conjurors, the final resort of desperately troubled people, disappeared during the post-war period. In March 1961 The Times reported that Wales' last *conjyr* was dead. According to an ethnographer from the Welsh Folk Museum, the man in question was a 'combination of wizard and quack doctor', with a lucrative gift for lifting spells and curing cattle of the evil eye. Before his death some two years earlier this conjyr had, in accordance with tradition, named a successor; but his apprentice too had since passed away. For good or ill, conjurors had gone from Wales.[18]

Notes

1 He may of course have specified that Hope was in Flintshire because it was not a well-known place, whereas the large town of Wrexham needed no reference to its county. I am assuming, along with Kate Bosse-Griffiths, that the author of the Llyfr Cyfrin is male. There is no hard evidence for this whatsoever but, even though there is a folktale account of Bela Fawr travelling some distance to perform magical work, it seems unlikely that a woman at that time would have been both literate and have had the freedom to travel unaccompanied to a male farmer. An educated woman would have been more constrained in her activities, while an uneducated woman would have been able to go where she was needed in rural settings but probably would not have had access to the written sources included in the Llyfr Cyfrin.
2 Summarised from *Hwyl* Cyf. I Rhif. 4–Rhagfyr 29 1883 p.55 https://journals.library.wales/view/2036853/2036905/6#?cv=6&m=3&h=beti%27r%2BOR%2Bbaten&xywh=2147%2C2551%2C1054%2C923
3 Suggett *A History of Magic and Witchcraft in Wales* p.88-89, 101, 103.
4 https://www.thesun.co.uk/news/13312968/couple-find-witchcraft-den-in-16th-century-home/
5 Bela Fawr is now most remembered incorrectly as the leader of the Llanddona witches. In Elias Owen p.223 an account of the witches of Llanddona follows his mention of Bela Fawr and the Denbigh witches. This must be the source of the tradition in which Bela was erroneously thought to be one of the Llanddona witches. This is found in the story Goronwy Tudor and the Witches of Llanddona in *The Welsh Fairy Book*, easily available on the Internet and the source of many retellings.
6 Edwards 1839 p. 60.
7 Foulkes, Isaac. 'Dyffryn clwyd: ei ramantau a'i Lafar Gwlad' *Transactions of the Cymmrodorion Society Sessions 1892-3* p. 88-103.
8 Suggett *History* p.98)
9 Edward Pugh, *Cambria Depicta: a Tour Through North Wales: Illustrated with Picturesque Views* (Williams, 1816) 391-392
10 Evans 1906: 127–29.
11 *Ancient and Modern Denbigh* 200 to 201.
12 Thomas Waters, *Cursed Britain: A History of Witchcraft and*

Black Magic in Modern Times (Yale University Press, 2020) p. 91-92; Lisa Tallis *Preternature*.
13 Jenkyn, *The Welsh Fairy Book* p.170-171.
14 Cambrian, 1806, be. 26. quoted from 299-300 *Bye-Gones*. Oct. 3,1906, A Welsh Wizard.
15
16 https://www.ruabon.com/mochyn.html
(Dic Smot was Richard Morris, the Derbyshire conjuror who was renowned in Wales for decades after his death.)
17 Mary Lewes, *The Queer Side of Things* (Selwyn, 1923) p.153-154.
18 *Cursed Britain* p.202-203.

Siôn y Rhose

Upon Oct. 25, 1832.
And he told me that his son had being seven times with a wise man that was called Shon y rhose but no better and that he could not do the work three moons, and I persuaded that I should be cured in that time.

This passage is intriguing for many reasons, not least for the naming of a 'wise man' that was called 'Shon y rhose'. (As there are several spellings for this name I will use the standard modern welsh form 'Siôn' except for quotations.) The author of Llyfr Cyfrin relishes Siôn's failure in lifting the witchcraft that affects the cattle. Farmer Allwood's son consulted him seven times, probably with payment each time, with no success. 'that he could not do the work three moons' suggests that Siôn would wait for the appropriate lunar cycle before working magic. Notably, 'wise man' is the English-language equivalent of dyn hysbys and the author of Llyfr Cyfrin is willing to grant him that title despite Siôn's lack of success.

The English of the journal entry is a little garbled, with 'being' instead of 'been' several times, consistent with someone whose first language is Welsh not English.

A search through Google and the National Library of Wales Welsh Journals and Welsh Newspapers sites drew a blank either for 'Shon y Rhose' or any variant. It was seeming likely that Siôn was lost to history, as many Welsh cunning folk must have been. Then, while searching for other material on Welsh cunning folk, I came across the following in the antiquarian periodical *Bye-Gones* of Aug. 29,

> There were several persons in North Wales about the first quarter of the present century pretending to be astrologers and to practise sortilege. Among the most noted were Mochyn Nant (Pig of the Dingle), John Evans, keeper of Elian's Well, Shon Rhosesmor, Bella, Sionet Gorn, and Sydney of Denbigh, Mary the White Mantle, and Shon Gyfarwydd of Llanbrynmair.[1]

Mochyn y Nant was a famous conjuror and fortune teller in Montgomeryshire for whom we have a good amount of information, including a notorious visit by the English literateur Thomas de Quincey. Bella, Sionet and Sydney are familiar from our account of characters in Denbighshire, as is John Evans who was the guardian of Ffynnon Elian cursing well. Mary the White Mantle or Mari y Fantell Wen was an unorthodox religious figure, and we will touch on Siôn Gyfarwydd in the next chapter. Siôn Rhosesmor, however, was looking very promising.

In another issue of *Bye-Gones*,

> There were other noted wells, viz., Ffynon Tegla, Llandegla, and the one at Rhosesmor, near Mold, kept by an old shoe maker, who met with a similar fate to that of the keeper of St. Elian's well, at Flint Castle.[2]

While it's possible that Siôn had his own well, the reference to a well at Rhosesmor is probably mistaken, as Siôn Rhosesmor was associated with Ffynnon Elian.

Siôn became notorious in 1819 when he was tried for receiving payment for lifting a curse at Ffynnon Elian. He was not tried under any witchcraft legislation, simply for fraud.

The main deponent was named John Pierce. He met John Edwards, Siôn Rhosesmor:-

> I saw John Edwards at his own house, called Berthddu, in the parish of Northop the area of Flintshire in which Rhosesmor was located, in the month of April, 1815. I understood I had been put in Fynnon Elian; I mean my name had been put in. I thought something was the matter with me. I saw every thing going cross. I was informed that John Edwards pulled people out of the well; I went to him in order to be pulled out. I told him something was the matter with me. He immediately observed my name was put in Fynnon Elian. I trembled! He said it was not then a fit time to take my name out, but desired me to wait till the next full moon, when he would take me out. He requested me in the interim to read the following Psalms: 6, 7, 20, 68, 109, and 118; afterwards he would let me know when to go to Fynnon Elian, as there were other people to go with us–it was absolutely necessary to go there. I went to his house in May following, to inquire about the proper time to go to the well. He said he would go on the following Sunday, and desired me to meet him at St. Asaph. We met there at seven o'clock on the Sunday evening; it was then full moon. Edwards fixed the day.[3]

Psalms were often read as a form of protective magic. What is particularly interesting is that Siôn (John Edwards) insisted on waiting for the next full moon. Lunar timing was also used by him when he tried to cure farmer Allwood's cattle, saying that he could not try again for three moons.

Edwards required that Pierce should pay him 15 shilling, but he was a few pennies short and could only pay 14s 6d. 15 shillings was a substantial amount of money at the time, representing more than a week's pay for a labourer. The other men, each of whom wanted some benefit from lifting curses, also paid Edwards.

We arrived there from 12 to half-past 12 on Sunday night; I never saw the well before; Edwards called me to the well, and showed it me; we went to a stile near the well; he bid us three go over and remain there till he fetched the key from the house where the woman of the well lived. He told me he would then pay the woman; he did not say where the house was; the well was inside a fence; I did not see a key; there was no door on it to my knowledge. Edwards was absent about 10 minutes; when he returned he desired one of the men to follow him; one of the strangers went with him; they were absent about a quarter of an hour or 20 minutes; when the man returned, I went in his stead. I found Edwards at the well; he bid me stand on one side of the well, and say the Lord's Prayer; I did so; he then emptied the well with a small wooden cup; when emptying it, he prayed to Father, Son, and Holy Ghost; the well then filled again. He then put some water into the cup, and desired me to drink some of it, and throw the remainder over my head; he said I must do so three times; I complied: after this, Edwards said, now we will look for your name. He put his hand a little above, near where the water goes into the well; he found something immediately, and said, 'Here is something,' which he gave to me. He desired me to put my hand in. I did so, but could find nothing. What he gave me was a piece of slate, a cork, a piece of sheet-lead, rolled up and tied together with a wire. I did not open it till I got home; it was in my possession till then. When I opened the sheet-lead, I found a piece of parchment inside, with the letters E. P. upon it; there were also some crosses.

The lifting of the curse was performed at midnight on a full moon with the recitation of prayers, including the Lord's prayer, and Pierce had three times to drink well water from a wooden cup and tip it over his head. The curse tablet was then removed from the well. Another account describes a room at Ffynnon Elian full of cursing tablets with initials. The skeptical have surmised that there was one for every common combination of initials.

Pierce couldn't say whether his lot had improved after the slate was taken from thee well. Margaret Pritchard, who had been keeper of the well at the time but had by then moved to Caernarvonshire, denied seeing Edwards at that time and had not met with him in person for three years, she said. Edwards was convicted, had to pay back the money, and was sentenced to be confined in the county gaol for twelve months.

Siôn y Rhose was later accused, in 1828, of gaining £5 by deception from Sarah Reece of Gwersyllt near Wrexham by using witchcraft and playing cards.[4] The evidence tells us that Siôn Rhosesmor's magical work was felt by his customers to be ineffective. He lifted supposed curses for four men who sued him, told the fortune for a woman who also sued him, and tried seven times to unwitch the cattle of Mr Allwood. We might hope that he was a better shoemaker than he was a dyn hysbys.

Notes

1 'Welsh Astrologers, Sorcerers', *Bye-Gones*. 1888. p.177
2 *Bye-Gones* Aug. 29, 1888, p. 179)
3 The report of the trial was first printed in Welsh in *Yr Eurgrawn Wesleaidd* 1819 p.58-6. In English, in a slightly curtailed form, it was printed decades later in the periodical *Cabinet of Curiosities*, No. 9, p. 137. This was reproduced in *Bye-Gones* (May 7, 1873) p. 185-186. It was also included in the 1852 English book *The Lives and Portraits of Curious and Odd Characters Compiled from Authentic Sources* (Worcester: Thomas Drew, 1852) in the chapter 'Edwards, the Welch Conjuror'.
4 Suggett *History* p.89

Siôn Gyfarwydd

The author of Llyfr Cyfrin is anonymous. All we know of him is that he was present in Wrexham in 1832 meeting farmer Allwood and then helping him at his farm in Flintshire. He may be one of the many dynion hysbys whose names are lost to time. However, if he does happen to be a figure who was remembered in print, who might he be?

We do know for certain that he was not the well-attested dyn hysbys Siôn y rhoses/Siôn Rhosesmor as he is referred to in the Llyfr Cyfrin itself.

One possibility is E. Edwards of Llwynybrain in Denbighshire, who was mentioned in the chapter on healing bewitched cattle. He successfully broke a spell which was preventing milk from being churned at Foel Fawr, Derwen. However, I have not been able to discover anything more about him than that his first name was Edward, along with some details of his family. An 1877 obituary of Margaret Edwards, Tyddyn Isaf states that she was married to John Edwards, son of Edward Edwards, Llwynybrain. It is not clear whether Edward Edwards would have been practising in 1832, but it is a possibility as his daughter-in-law Margaret was born in 1830 and if her husband John was of a somewhat similar age to her then his father Edward would necessarily have been an adult in 1832.

There are other possibilities.

Included in the list of famous magical practitioners in north Wales in the first quarter of the nineteenth century is one Siôn Gyfarwydd of Llanbrynmair. We know a good deal about him from folklore and other sources.

The word cyfarwydd is used in modern Welsh with the meaning 'common'. It does have a variety of other meanings. *Geiriadur Prifysgol Cymru* offers:-

> well-informed, acquainted, familiar; learned, versed, expert, skilful, proficient; well-known; skilled in magic, &c

Gŵr cfarwydd was synonymous with dyn hysbys. This last meaning is obviously the prime intention for the epithet, yet it also had the implication of Siôn the expert, or Siôn the learned (the initial 'c' has mutated into 'G' as epithets take a soft mutation in Welsh.) His given name was John Roberts and he was remembered decades later not only for his craft as a gŵr cyfarwydd but as a bookbinder.[1]

This was a somewhat more respectable profession than being a shoemaker (as was Siôn Rhosesmor) or a tailor. Siôn Gyfarwydd probably died around 1860, give or take a couple of years, but he was remembered for decades afterwards.

> It would be interesting if a full list could be compiled of the old Welsh bookbinders. The art of "casing" books was very often learnt and practised by Nonconformist ministers as a means of eking out a livelihood. . . Among the laymen who followed the craft may be named Thomas Baxter of Llanfair, and John Roberts.[2]

According to History of the Parish of Llanbrynmair,

> The belief in conjuring was also formerly very general. The last professor of the black art in this parish was Mr.

John Roberts (Sion Gyfarwydd), who was also a bookbinder, and who died from twenty-five to thirty years ago. Some persons may still be found who believe in conjuring.³

Kate Bosse-Griffiths gives another reference by the dyn hysbys to a manuscript that 'on p. 41-42 is noted a method "To cure witchcraft" that has been quoted from the Blackgrave MSS.' Annoyingly, she does not include the spell. Another spell is titled, 'Another strange necromantic spell "from a curious manuscript"' – these are from *The Familiar Astrologer*.

My research has shown that in addition to unknown or uncertain sources, the author of Llyfr Cyfrin has included material from *The Familiar Astrologer* (1828) by Robert Cross Smith (Raphael), from which the above legendary charm derives.

Siôn was a bookman and bibliophile. He is among the list of subscribers for two different literary publications, *Blodau Glyn Dyfi* (1852) and *Geirionydd: cyfansoddiadau barddonol, cerddorol, a rhyddieithol y diweddar E. Evans* (1862.)⁴

While it is true that we do not know the name of the author of Llyfr Cyfrin with any certainty, I would tentatively suggest that Siôn Gyfarwydd is the author. We might wonder if he bound the Llyfr Cyfrin himself, given Kate Bosse-Griffiths' vivid description of it.

There is no hard evidence for my cautious identification of Siôn Gyfarwydd – or anyone else – as the author, but he is a good fit. It may be objected that Siôn lived quite far away from Wrexham, in Llanbrynmair west of Machynlleth. Yet we have seen how Siôn Rhosesmor travelled about 50 miles to Ffynnon Elian to lift the supposed curses placed on Edward Pierce and his friends. Also, an 1870 reminiscence of the dynion hysbys earlier in the century stated,

Tystiai 'Jac Ffynnon Elian,' a 'Sion Gyfarwydd,' fod eu cwsmeriaid goreu yn dyfod o Loegr.[5]

'Jac Ffynnon Elian,' and 'Sion Gyfarwydd,' testified that their best customers came from England.'

In 1915 'D.R.T.' could still write, 'Quite recently, I have known another farmer take a journey of many miles to consult a Wise Man" in the neighbourhood of Llanidloes about some bullocks he had lost.'[6]

Further, three tales about Siôn Gyfarwydd were told to Elias Owen by Mr. Jones, Rector of Bylchau, near Denbigh, showing that Siôn's reputation was remembered in Denbighshire long after the 1830s. So there is no compelling reason to believe that Siôn could not have travelled to Wrexham to meet the farmer, as the town would have been somewhat midway between Hope, Flintshire and Llanbrynmair. In one of the stories below, Siôn treated a publican in Llanfyllin, which is 25 miles away and halfway to Wrexham.

Siôn Gyfarwydd and the author of Llyfr Cyfrin both have a strong interest in books; both were successful cattle healers; both had clientele from beyond their immediate vicinities (he met Flintshire farmer Allwood in Wrexham), both were active in the 1830s. It may be objected that many dynion hysbys healed cattle and liked books. Yet there were also those who were unsuccessful or fraudulent, like Siôn Rhosesmor, and who have no recorded interest in books, also like Siôn Rhosesmor.

Siôn Gyfarwydd certainly had a long-lasting reputation. Unlike Siôn Rhosesmor, whose name has been preserved to history for two cases of fraud and another in which his magic was ineffective, Siôn Gyfarwydd was mostly renowned for success in his practices. To my knowledge he does not appear in any court records. Each of the following stories resembles a believable anecdote rather than a fantastical and fabulous folktale.

Even if Siôn might turn out not to have been the author of Llyfr Cyfrin, the author was someone like him, and these tales cast light on the activities of dynion hysbys at the time.

Elias Owen devotes an unusual amount of space to him:-

> R. H., a farmer in Llansilin parish, who lost several head of cattle, sent or went to Shon Gyfarwydd, who lived in Llanbrynmair, a well-known conjuror, for information concerning their death, and for a charm against further loss. Both were obtained, and the charm worked so well that the grateful farmer sent a letter to Shon acknowledging the benefit he had derived from him.
>
> This Shon was a great terror to thieves, for he was able to spot them and mark them in such a way that they were known to be culprits. I am indebted to Mr. Jones, Rector of Bylchau, near Denbigh, for the three following stories, in which the very dread of being marked by Shon was sufficient to make the thieves restore the stolen property.
>
> STOLEN PROPERTY DISCOVERED THROUGH FEAR OF APPLYING TO THE LLANBRYNMAIR CONJUROR.
>
> Richard Thomas, Post Office, Llangadfan, lost a coat and waistcoat, and he suspected a certain man of having stolen them. One day this man came to the shop, and Thomas saw him there, and, speaking to his wife from the kitchen in a loud voice, so as to be heard by his customer in the shop, he said that he wanted the loan of a horse to go to Llanbrynmair. Llanbrynmair was, as we know, the conjuror's place of abode. Thomas, however, did not leave his house, nor did he intend doing so, but that very night the stolen property was returned, and it was found the next morning on the door sill.
>
> RECLAIMING STOLEN PROPERTY THROUGH FEAR OF THE CONJUROR.
>
> A mason engaged in the restoration of Garthbeibio Church placed a trowel for safety underneath a stone, but by morning it was gone. Casually in the evening he

informed his fellow workmen that he had lost his trowel, and that someone must have stolen it, but that he was determined to find out the thief by taking a journey to Llanbrynmair. He never went, but the ruse was successful, for the next morning he found, as he suspected would be the case, the trowel underneath the very stone where he had himself placed it.

ANOTHER SIMILAR TALE.

Thirty pounds were stolen from Glan-yr-afon, Garthbeibio. The owner made known to his household that he intended going to Shon the conjuror, to ascertain who had taken his money, but the next day the money was discovered, being restored, as was believed, by the thief the night before.

These stories show that the ignorant and superstitious were influenced through fear, to restore what they had wrongfully appropriated, and their faith in the conjuror's power thus resulted, in some degree, in good to the community. The *Dyn Hyspys* was feared where no one else was feared, and in this way the supposed conjuror was not altogether an unimportant nor unnecessary member of society. At a time, particularly when people are in a low state of civilization, or when they still cling to the pagan faith of their forefathers, transmitted to them from remote ages, then something can be procured for the good of a benighted people even through the medium of the *Gŵr Cyfarwydd*.[7]

Not all recollections of Siôn were positive. Many enquiries into magic and folklore were motivated by simple curiosity about Welsh traditions and reminiscence, but others came from the perspective either of Victorian rationalism or a nonconformist religious suspicion of witchcraft and magic.

Many years ago a publican at Llanfyllin, who was suffering severely from erysipelas in his knee, believed that he had been witched by an elderly widow, who was then residing "in that peaceful little town." All the doctors in the neighbourhood tried their best to alleviate his pains, but without success. He could not banish from his mind the appearance of the old lady when he refused giving her chips, and continued to believe that she was the cause of all his sufferings. However, at last, a small farmer in the neighbourhood was sent to "Shon Gyfarwydd, the wise astrologer of Llanbrynmair," who, in the language of Shakespeare, could Call spirits from the vasty deep. The farmer, after gravely consulting the oracle, returned, when a cockerel was immediately procured, and was tied in his feathers around the sufferer's knee. They afterwards sent for the old woman Price to give her blessing on their doings. The bird was kept on the joiner's knee for several days without effecting a cure. The patient was taken afterwards to Shrewsbury Infirmary, where death put an end to his misery and superstition.'[8]

At that time in the rural areas there was a strong belief in witchcraft, or the art of harmful magic [rheibio]. There was no Llan or village without a witch or wizard. And he was capable of cursing [rheibio] man and beast, if they were not in the particular way under the protection of the planets, and the conjuror was considered one of the most important and most vital men in the land. A certain disease afflicted the animals at Tyddyn Noddfa, and the mare, and many of the pigs, calves, and various geese, died. Mrs Cyfeiliog claimed that they had been looked crossly upon and bewitched; and there was to be no peace for Tudor without resorting to Shon Gyfarwydd, so that he might unwitch the animals, and set them under the protection of the planets. Tudur went, and Shon Gyfarwydd did his job effectively. He made a paper parchment for him to take home, ordering him to put it in a glass bottle and to seal the cork on it. Everything was done correctly according to instructions, and everything at Tyddyn Noddfa was a great success. Hywel insisted on opening the bottle on one of his visits to his home, but there was nothing written on it except the signs of the planets. But, nevertheless, the old people wanted the paper to have some charm and protective virtue that could which could paralyse every witchery (rhaib) cast upon men, animals, and possessions.[9]

He seemed to have become almost proverbial in his ability to answer quesions. This article in *Y Punch Cymraeg* of 1858 looks humorously at the notion of a machine that can answer questions.

> Gan mai offeryn Celfyddydawl yn siarad yn ddamegol heb dafod yw'r Peiriant, dylai pawb fod fel Sion Cyfarwydd–yn alluog i ddeall ei atebion heb unrhyw eglureb.

> Since the Machine is a mechanical instrument speaking metaphorically without a tongue, everyone should be like Sion Cyfarwydd–able to understand its answers without any explanation.[10]

In an 1888 article recalling 'Welsh Astrologers, Sorcerers &c.' in the antiquarian magazine *By-Gones*, he is considered the end of a tradition 'The last of this race was old John Roberts, Shôn Gyfarwydd, who died a few years ago at Llanbrynmair.'

Perhaps he was indeed among the last of those conjurors, dynion hysbys and menywod hysbys and diviners who attained the kind of renown which reached its apogee in the figure of John Harries, charms and unwitching and cattle healing other forms of folk magic were current in rural Wales into the middle of the twentieth century.

Notes

1 There was even another renowned Welsh wizard with the same name. The given name of the celebrated conjuror Mochyn y Nant was also John Roberts. These anglicized names were very popular in Wales in the nineteenth century. A limited number of forenames were typically used in combination with a limited number of surnames. Thus there were John Roberts and Mary Joneses galore. Epithets such as the name of the house or farm where the person lived, or of some distinguishing characteristic or profession were needed to distinguish one John Roberts from the other. This practice persisted when communities became anglicized, famously resulting in comical nicknames like the undertaker Dai the Death. In the case of Siôn Gyfarwydd the Welsh version of his forename and his profession of Cyfarwydd was enough to distinguish him from all the John Roberts, just as Shon Rhosesmor was John Edwards plus his locale.
2 (Sion Gyfarwydd), of Llanbrynmair. Aug. 13, 1890. *Bye-Gones.* 431 '...Llanbrynmair developed around the Wynnstay Arms at Pen-y-Bont on the main road between Caersws and Machynlleth.' *Dictionary of the Place-Names of Wales* p. 222.
3 Robert Williams, "A History of the Parish of Llanbrynmair." *Montgomeryshire Collections*, Vol. 22, 1888, p. 326
Richard Suggett surmised, 'Some conjurors, like Siôn Gyfarwydd who was also a bookbinder, lived surrounded by books, and others had specialist libraries.' Suggett p. 86.
Suggett also points out that 'An antiquarian interest in the conjuror's art is shown by the copy of a "A legendary charm used in former days in gathering herbs" taken from "an old black letter missal in possession of the mercury "Suggett p.100
4 List of subscribers p. 463
Roberts, Mr. John, bookbinder, Llanbrynmair
5 *Cronicl y cymdeithasau crefyddol* Cyf. XXVIII rhif. 322–Chwefror 1870 p.54 https://journals.library.wales/view/1238716/1240391/176
6 D.R.T. 'Demonology and Witchcraft' in *Collections, historical & archaeological relating to Montgomeryshire* vol 37 p. 145; 7 (Elias Owen *Welsh Folklore* p. 258-).
8 *Bye-Gones.* Aug., 1883 p. 282
9 My translation
Y winllan cylchgrawn misol y Wesleyaid vol 51 rhif 8 Awst 1898

Hywel Cyfeiliog. VI.–'Ofergoelion Y Dyddiau Gynt', 'Superstitions of Days Gone-by'.
10 *Y Punch Cymraeg* 20th March 1858 p.4
https://journals.library.wales/
view/2139555/2139604/3#?xywh=-2122%2C-
260%2C7882%2C5198

Bewitched Cattle

A farmer from the parish of Hope, Flintshire, met with me in Wrexham. And complained much that his cattle and milk had been witched. And that some of the cattle had lost their dids. I asked him how long had it being so. He told me between two and three months and his loss was very great, and that all his cheese were spoilt. . . Accordingly I did through God's assistance to the great astonishment and satisfaction of the Farmer and his family. For they told me that the first cheese that was made after was richer and better than could be expected.

Cattle healing was a major function of the dyn hysbys. As the grandson of a Welsh vet

> Grandfather Lloyd had been a veterinary surgeon in the late 1800s in this rural part of Wales and he could relate many examples of cases where animals had dropped dead, for no apparent reason, and where on the same farms the cream had obstinately refused to turn to butter in the churn. In such cases, where the veterinary surgeon was unable to help, the local conjuror or wise man would be summoned . . .[1]

We do not know what method the dyn hysbys used to unwitch Farmer Allwood's cattle. The Llyfr Cyfrin is not a transcription of all methods used by this particular dyn hysbys but a collection of material he had found in the course of his researches and thought worthy to copy down. If the unwitching method was actually included in the Llyfr Cyfrin it is likely that Kate Bosse-Griffiths neglected to record it because it was in English. She does however include the reference to a spell '"To Cure Witchcraft" taken from the Blackgrave MSS.' I have not been able to trace the source for this, and the Blackgrave MSS are otherwise unknown, but it seems more likely that the dyn hysbys found this witchcraft cure in a printed book rather than in the Blackgrave MSS themselves.

It is more likely that the dyn hysbys used one of the techniques that have been recorded by Welsh folklorists. Whatever approach may have been used, it seems that the focus was on curing the cattle, not on identifying the perpetrator of the bewitching. This may have been a cultural tendency. Just as there were historically few witchcraft accusations in Wales, cunning men may have been reluctant to identify witches as the process would have stirred up a good deal of bad feeling in the community.

There were, however, occasional attempts by conjurors to identity the individuals who caused the bewitching. This practice was risky as a precise yet incorrect identification was clearly derogatory and could result in a slander case or in violent reprisal. A loose description was safer than a name (without taking into account that it was easier to magically scry the image of a person than obtain a name and address) especially if it could refer to a handful of people.

Wales had never been consumed by a craze for witch hunting to the extent that England, and more so Scotland, had. Yet there were plenty of cases of witch accusations which made their way to the slander courts. Even in the time of the Denbighshire dyn hysbys vindictive and unfair witch accusations could be made. In 1827 in Llanfoist near Abergavenny a farmer William Watkin blamed 90-year-old Mary Nicholas for the severe losses to his cattle herd. Mary was dragged to the dead animals by the parish constable and a couple of

Watkins' servants.

> Meanwhile, a crowd of perhaps one hundred gathered. Mr Watkins made Mary kneel behind a colt, take hold of the animal's tail, and pray for the Almighty to bless the cattle. As Mary made her recitations, he pulled a briar rose from a nearby hedge. The farmer walked to where the old woman knelt and drew the thorns across her arm, with the idea that spilling the old witch's blood would diffuse her magic.[2]

Mary was then stripped naked and in the absence of witch marks on her body they found what was presumably a growth on her head which they cut off along with her hair.

Mary successfully took the farmer and his allies to court where they were found guilty of assault. The prosperous and 'respectable' farmer succeeded in commuting the sentence via a petition which was signed by some of the local great and the good, including 'three surgeons, three lawyers, a magistrate and a general.'

It is notable that no cunning man or conjuror was involved in this horrible example. The emphasis was all on scapegoating a poor old woman rather than obtaining a cure.

Occasionally a witch might be blamed for physically invading the milk churn.

> Until very lately I had thought that the milk only was considered bewitched if it could not be churned, and not that the witch herself was at the bottom of the churn. But I have been disabused of this false notion, for the Rector of Llanycil told me the following story, which was told him by his servant girl, who figures in the tale. When this girl was servant at Drws-y-nant, near Dolgelley, one day, the milk would not churn. They worked a long time at it to no purpose. The girl thought that she heard something knocking up and down in the churn, and splashing about. She told her master there was something in

the churn, but he would not believe her; however, they removed the lid, and out jumped a large hare, and ran away through the open door, and this explained all difficulties, and proved that the milk was bewitched, and that the witch herself was in the churn in the shape of a hare.

This girl affirmed that she had seen the hare with her own eyes.[3]

These operations were often complex and the dyn hysbys may have used a combination of techniques, perhaps augmenting the curing of the cattle with charms and rituals designed to prevent further witchcraft.

A survey of material follows, a fairly full selection of the available material. At the end I will suggest that a symbol from Llyfr Cyfrin, included almost incidentally by Kate Bosse-Griffiths, may be associated with surviving charms discovered in Powys and may indicate part of our dyn hysbys's method of curing and preventing witchcraft-induced cattle sickness.

Possibly the earliest account of a Welsh animal healing is by Edward Savage (1759-1849). In this case he was healing a pig.

> The following incident, related by a highly respectable and trustworthy person as a 'remarkable coincidence which I cannot explain,' will show the nature of the old conjuror's method of procedure, and the means by which he earned his money and his fame. The father of the narrator had lost one valuable pig from disease, and a second was purchased in his place, which was suddenly taken ill, and for days would eat nothing. Some of the credulous neighbours at once suggested that human agency had something to do with the pig's illness, in fact, that it was 'witched.' The young man resolved to secretly visit 'Old Savage,' and elicit his opinion, with no great faith in the result. Carrying his resolution into effect, he arrived at the conjuror's house and stated his errand to the

wise man, who at once consulted his books, wrote out a charm, and gave him some herbs to mingle with the pig's food. He also gave him particular directions regarding the charm, and described its immediate effect upon the patient, and further stated that the cause of his sufferings resided between the young man's home and the north, and that she should not rest during the night if his advice was carefully attended to. Savage's directions were duly carried out, the paper upon whicn the charm was written was rubbed over the pig from head to tail the prescribed number of times, and then placed for his further protection in a crack in the wall of his cot. Some of his bristles were then taken, placed between two flat irons, and put on the top of the fire, where they remained all night. On the following morning, to the utter astonishment of the operator, a neighbour who lived only a few doors to the north came into the house as the family were at breakfast, and complained that she had not rested during the night, having suffered acutely from tooth-ache. The spell was broken, the pig recovered, and knew no more suffering till placed in the hands of the butcher.[4]

Perhaps the most apropos of all these cases, at least in terms of time and geography, comes from Elias Owen. This took place in Denbighshire but it may well have been later in the century than 1832, the year in which our dyn hysbys performed his cattle unwitching.

> Mrs. Susan Williams, Garth, a farm on the confines of Efenechtyd parish, Denbighshire, told the writer that E. Edwards, Llwynybrain, Gwyddelwern, was famous for breaking spells, and consequently his aid was often required. Susan stated that they could not churn at Foel Fawr, Derwen. They sent for Edwards, who came, and offered up a kind of prayer, and then placed a ring made of the bark or of the wood of the mountain ash (she could not recollect which) underneath the churn, or the lid of the churn, and thus the spell was broken.[5]

These preventative methods using branches of particular trees were also attested in Cardiganshire.

The belief in witchcraft in connection with agricultural pursuits was also very strong. If milk turned sour or cream would not churn, it was believed to be bewitched. Also tales of bewitched pigs, sheep, cows, and other farm animals are recorded. Bewitched milk and milk products were remedied by putting a branch of rowan tree or mountain ash over the door of the dairy or by putting a knife into the milk or cream—for witches like fairies hated iron.[6]

Service magicians in Wales were generally more concerned with using ritual methods to remove the bewitchment, and thus heal the cattle, than they were to hunt out the perpetrator. In one of the examples below the farmer suspected two people in turn of bewitching the cattle but the conjuror focused instead on the ritual method of plunging a red hot poker into the cream and ignored the identity of the supposed witch.

In contrast, the retrieval of stolen goods would almost certainly require knowledge of the thief as the thief would be in possession of the stolen property or would know its location. Cattle bewitching and unwitching could, like cursing, be understood to exist in a completely magical context. If a menyw hysbys revealed who had stolen a purse the remedy (divination of the person and the location) was magical but the offending act was not, it was merely theft. If cattle were understood to have been bewitched the very act of bewitching was itself harmful magic. These days we separate the misfortunes of theft and sick cattle quite differently: the former belongs to human criminality, the latter to natural causes. If an annual fee paid to the conjuror to replace and renew a charm is understood to keep the milk flowing bountifully and the butter churning effortlessly, who is to complain?

Detection has much in common with other objects of

divination such as finding the identity of a thief, yet by their nature witches may be more difficult to discover and their malevolent powers may confer additional risk.

While the methods for unwitching cattle are many, there may be considered to be three aspects to the problem:
1. Curing the cattle (and the dairy products)
2. Preventing further bewitching
3. Identifying the perpetrator.

These may all be connected: a cure may depend on finding a cause, in this case the witch (or possibly the fairies or other sources of bad luck.)

Prevention is always easier and more desirable than cure. To quote a tale of the esteemed Mullah Nasruddin,

> Mullah Nasruddin is both a fool and a wise man. He was out one day in his garden sprinkling bread crumbs around the flowerbeds. A neighbor came by and asked, 'Mullah, why are you doing that?'
> Nasruddin answered, 'Oh, I do it to keep the tigers away.'
> The neighbor said, 'But there aren't any tigers within thousands of miles of here.'
> Nasruddin replied, 'Effective, isn't it?'[7]

Another very apropos story, referring both to cattle bewitching and unwitching and to Denbighshire, involves our old friend Bela Fawr. It is again recounted by Elias Owen. Just as the author of Llyfr Cyfrin was asked to unwitch the cattle of Farmer Allwood only after Shon y Rhoses had been unsuccessful, so Bela Fawr was called in once a Pwllheli conjuror had failed to help.

> Before beginning this tale, it should be said that some witches were able to make void the curses of other witches. Bella of Denbigh, who lived in the early part of the present century, was one of these, and her renown extended over many counties.

I may further add that my informant is the Rev. R. Jones, whom I have often mentioned, who is a native of Llanfrothen, the scene of the occurrences I am about to relate, and that he was at one time curate of Denbigh, so that he would be conversant with the story by hearsay, both as to its evil effects and its remedy.

About the year 1815 an old woman, supposed to be a witch, lived at Ffridd Ucha, Llanfrothen, and she got her living by begging. One day she called at Ty mawr, in the same parish, requesting a charity of milk; but she was refused. The next time they churned, the milk would not turn to butter, they continued their labours for many hours, but at last they were compelled to desist in consequence of the unpleasant odour which proceeded from the churn. The milk was thrown away, and the farmer, John Griffiths, divining that the milk had been witched by the woman who had been begging at their house, went to consult a conjuror, who lived near Pwllheli. This man told him that he was to put a red hot crowbar into the milk the next time they churned. This was done, and the milk was successfully churned. For several weeks the crowbar served as an antidote, but at last it failed, and again the milk could not be churned, and the unpleasant smell made it again impossible for anyone to stand near the churn. Griffiths, as before, consulted the Pwllheli conjuror, who gave him a charm to place underneath the churn, stating, when he did so, that if it failed, he could render no further assistance. The charm did not act, and a gentleman whom he next consulted advised him to go to Bell, or Bella, the Denbigh witch. Griffiths did so, and to his great surprise he found that Bell could describe the position of his house, and she knew the names of his fields. Her instructions were – Gather all the cattle to Gors Goch field, a meadow in front of the house, and then she said that the farmer and a friend were to go to a certain holly tree, and stand out of sight underneath this tree, which to this day stands in the hedge that surrounds the meadow mentioned by Bell. This was to be done by night, and the farmer was told that he should then see the person who had injured him. The instructions were literally carried out. When the cows came to the field they herded together in a frightened manner, and commenced bellowing fearfully. In a very short time, who should enter the field but the suspected woman in evident bodily pain, and Griffiths and his friend heard her uttering some words unintelligible to them, and having done so, she disappeared, and the cattle became quiet, and ever after they had no difficulty in churning the milk of those cows.[8]

One common method was to put a red hot poker or crowbar into the milk, although this was often accompanied by other techniques. It's tempting to see this as a primitive form of pasteurisation, but it's unlikely that anything like full pasteurisation could have been produced. Perhaps the red hot iron was simply understood to repel witches.

WITCHCRAFT ON THE WELSH BORDER.—A Pall Mall Gazette correspondent writes:—In the Western Counties of England the belief in witchcraft is still very common. Some two years ago I was fishing on the border of Wales, and got as a companion and guide an old man who had formerly been a painter and glazier, but had now given up work. For the first few days we had fair sport, and then, as often happens, the fish would not rise to any fly whatever we put on, probably owing to there being no hatch-out of the natural insects. I said to the old man: 'I shall chuck it for a day or two; there may be thunder in the air.' To which he replied, gravely: 'No, sir, it is not that: I broke the top of my rod this morning, which I have not done for years, and I got a beautiful lot of worms which they won't look at; but I think I know the party as has overlooked me; she's a palsied one and all of a tremble.' When I ventured to doubt the old lady's power, he said it was all mentioned in the Bible, therefore there could be no doubt on the subject. I questioned the landlord of the inn afterwards. He told me it was the general belief, that only a fortnight before a farmer in the neighbourhood, whose pig had died and butter would not come, had gone ten miles to pay and consult a conjuror. 'What did he tell you?' asked the landlord. 'He said I must tell my wife to put a red-hot poker in the churn, and the person who had bewitched me was not the party I thought, but a sandy-haired one who lived a mile from my house.' 'And did the butter come then?' asked the landlord. 'It did,' said the man, 'in twenty minutes; but however could the conjuror have told it was that sandy-haired party as done me all the mischief?'[9]

The use of written charms is widely attested and was a mainstay in cattle healing and protection. There are long charms in Welsh manuscripts from the sixteenth century for protecting cattle from bewitchment and from disease, and this was still a thriving industry in the nineteenth century.

I have also known a Nonconformist deacon who went regularly to a Montgomeryshire magician, paying his ten shillings each time, to secure a charm when the farm churning went wrong or when one of his beasts had been bewitched. The charms are generally a garble of English words illegibly written in which the phrase In the name of the Father and of the Son and of the Holy Ghost predominates.[10]

Elias Owen offers an example of one of these charms as following:

CHARM AGAINST FOOT AND MOUTH DISEASE.

The cattle on a certain farm in Llansilin parish suffered from the above complaint, and old Mr. H--- consulted a conjuror, who gave him a written charm which he was directed to place on the horns of the cattle, and he was told this would act both as a preventive and a cure. This farmer's cattle might be seen with the bit of paper, thus procured, tied to their horns. My informant does not wish to be named, nor does she desire the farmer's name to be given, but she vouches for the accuracy of her information, and for my own use, she gave me all particulars respecting the above. This took place only a few years ago, when the Foot and Mouth Disease first visited Wales.

I obtained, through the kindness of the Rev. John Davies, vicar of Bryneglwys, the following charm procured from Mr. R. Jones, Tynywern, Bryneglwys, Denbighshire, who had it from his uncle, by whom it was used at one time.

Yn enw y Tad, a'r Mab, a'r Ysbryd.
Bod I grist Iesu y gysegredig a oddefe ar y groes,
Pan godaist Sant Lasarys o'i fedd wedi farw,
Pan faddeuaist Bechodau I fair fagdalen, a thrygra
wrthyf fel bo gadwedig bob peth a henwyf fi ag a
croeswyf fi ++++ trwy nerth a rhinwedd dy eiriau
Bendigedig di fy Arglwydd Iesu Crist. Amen.
Iesu Crist ain harglwydd ni gwared ni rhag pop
rhiwogaeth o Brofedigaeth ar yabrydol o uwch deiar
nag o Is deiar, rhag y gythraelig o ddun nei ddynes
a chalon ddrwg a reibia dda ei berchenog ei
ddrwg rhinwedd ei ddrwg galon ysgymynedig
a wahanwyd or ffydd gatholig ++++ trwy nerth a
rhinwedd dy eiriau Bendigedig di fy Arglwydd Iesu
Crist. Amen.
Iesu Crist ain harglwydd ni Gwared ni rhag y glwy
ar bar, ar Llid, ar genfigain ar adwyth . . .
ar Pleined Wibrenon ar gwenwyn
deiarol, trwy nerth a rhinwedd dy eiriau
Bendigedig di Fy Arglwydd Iesu Crist. Amen.

It was somewhat difficult to decipher the charms and four words towards the end are quite illegible, and consequently they are omitted. The following translation will show the nature of the charm:–

In the Name of the Father, the Son, and the Spirit.
May Christ Jesus the sanctified one, who suffered death on the cross,
When thou didst raise Lazarus from his tomb after his death,

When Thou forgavest sins to Mary Magdalen, have
mercy on me, so that everything named by me and
crossed by me ++++ may be saved by the power and
virtue of thy blessed words my Lord Jesus Christ.
Amen.
Jesus Christ our Lord save us from every kind of
temptation whether spiritual above the earth or
under the earth, from the devilish man or woman
with evil heart who bewitcheth the goods of their
owner; his evil virtue, his evil excommunicated heart
cut off from the Catholic Faith ++++ by the power
and virtue of thy blessed words my Lord Jesus Christ.
Amen.
Jesus Christ our Lord save us from the disease and
the affliction, and the wrath, and the envy, and the
mischief, and the . . . and the planet of the sky
and the earthly poison, by the power and virtue
of Thy blessed words, my Lord Jesus Christ. Amen.

The mark ++++ indicates that crosses were here made
by the person who used the charm, and probably the
words of the charm were audibly uttered.[11]

An unusually full account of cattle charming in Montgomeryshire is given here:-

> I shall now proceed to tell you a few stories regarding the first class of case about which the farmer consults the conjuror, namely regarding the animals. Perhaps many animals have died on a farm and the farmer, fearing all will die, hurriedly goes to the local conjuror to ask his advice about checking the trouble. As a rule, when the messenger arrives at the conjuror's house, he is asked what the trouble is, and the conjuror retires to consult his books. He usually consults two books placed side by side in his private room, one of which is usually an almanack. He then notes the days on which the different animals died, and then consults the other book, shaking his head, etc.
> He then returns to the messenger and gets him to promise on his oath that he will not mention a word of

his advice to anybody else. Then he will probably state that there is somebody in the neighbourhood who wishes all evil to him, and that it is the evil wish that has caused the trouble with the animals. The conjuror will then write on paper-firstly across the paper very closely, then down the paper, then across over this, until it is quite undecipherable. This he will put in a bottle which, as a rule, he seals with lead. He will then tell the messenger that this bottle must be placed in the cowhouse, stable, or pigsty, on one of the walls or under the roof. A highly respectable farmer informed me that he had bottles like this in all his outhouses and that he would never as long as he lived allow them to be moved. He believed that these bottles kept his farm free from all troubles. The charms vary.

I have seen several of these charms and have two in my possession. They are written very closely and are difficult to decipher. They were given to a farmer by a conjuror about four years ago. Both of them open thus, 'In the name of the Father and the Son and the Holy Ghost, Amen.' Then come three crosses and in the name of the Lord Jesus Christ his Redeemer and Saviour he will relieve So and So of So and So-his ewes and lambs and to bring them alright from all witchcraft, etc., etc., with several Amens placed after several sentences and three crosses after every Amen. At the bottom of the sheet on the left is the magical word Abracadabra written in triangular form. In the centre is a number of planetary symbols and on the right a circular figure filled in with various symbols; at the bottom in the centre is written May Jah Jah Jah.

There are, I believe, other charms in use for stopping bleeding in animals and for other diseases of animals and for diseases of all kinds in human beings. I am told that there was a charm for shingles and even for toothache.

About five years ago a conjuror was asked to visit a farm where many animals had died. He came there and asked the farmer to come with him to an adjoining field. After looking round for some time, he turned to the farmer and asked him where were the North, South, East, and West. The farmer indicated the points of the compass to him. The conjuror then drew an imaginary line from North to South, and another from East to West. Where the both lines crossed he ordered the farmer to dig a hole in the ground. Whilst the farmer was doing this, he was consulting a book which he took out of his pocket, He then wrote on a sheet of paper, inserted the paper in a bottle and put it in the hole which the farmer had dug. The earth was replaced, and the farmer informed me quite solemnly that not a single animal died afterwards. This is a very typical instance of how the Sign of the Cross comes in frequently in the use of remedies for combating evil doers and evil wishers. Compare also the use of the Cross on dough and on butter.

A parallel story to this is that of a farm where all the animals were dying very rapidly; geese, turkeys, and hens were dying one after another. The birds would run from each side of the yard to meet each other beak to beak and then drop dead. Matters came to a climax when a pony was found dead one morning on the top of the thrashing machine. No one could explain how the pony had managed to get to such a place. The conjuror was sent for and immediately made a post mortem of the pony and took out its heart. He then heated a long skewer in the kitchen fire. When the skewer had got white hot he plunged it into the heart, vertically and horizontally. Again, as you note, in this way making the Sign of the Cross.

I am informed that after this operation no further deaths occurred. This story has a feature common to most of these witchcraft stories of farm animals – the animals are found dead or may be alive in places that they could never have got to by themselves. This is a sure sign of witchcraft and has to be treated accordingly.

A farmer moved to a distant neighbourhood (he went from Montgomeryshire to Breconshire). Shortly after going there, his animals started dying, and the last animal to die was a cow. They had turned cattle out to drink at a brook and the cow fell so awkwardly that both horns went into the ground and she broke her neck. The owner hurried to the conjuror, who asked the farmer if he would know the man who had just left the farm, i.e., his immediate predecessor, if he saw him. The conjuror then showed him in a glass of water the father and daughter who had left the farm, and no more animals died.

In another case where animals were dying, the conjuror advised that, when the next animal died, its heart should be taken out and put in the oven after it had been heated. He told them that, after this was done, they would see the man who was causing the trouble come to the house, but he must not be admitted at any price. They must keep him locked out. After the heart was completely destroyed the trouble would cease, and so it did. A horse when at work was very lame on one of his forefeet. He was not lame when idle, and could run about in the yard or field without any lameness but put him to any work and he immediately became too lame to move. The conjuror was consulted and this was his advice: At mid-day to-morrow, remember, 12 o'clock exactly, take the horse out to the nearest field to the house. While the horse is standing, cut the sod around the hoof of the lame leg; get someone then to lift the leg, turn the sod with the earth upwards, and put the horse's foot back on this earth. I shall be in my room at the time. Keep the horse standing on this for ten minutes, and then take him back to the stable and all will be well. And so it was. In one district that I know very well, when one of the cattle gets lame from a kind of foot-rot which is rather common among the cattle, the farmer watches the animal treading in some soft ground. He notes carefully the mark made by the diseased foot. He then cuts around the mark and lifts the clod up. This he places on a blackthorn tree, and as it withers the diseased foot of the animal gets better. This is the regular practice in one district, and the farmers all believe it is a certain cure.[12]

Other methods used harmful countermagic to expose the perpetrators. (Harries Werndew was a different dyn hysbys to the more famous John Harries Cwrt-y-cadno.)

'That was about the time when we were losing cows at the Pant. A cow would become ill and by the morning it was dead, and no one could say why. And then I heard that the same thing was happening with William of Gelli, and I began to think that there was a bewitcher about, so I told William that we had better go to see Doctor Harries Werndew, the exorcist, and so we did. Harries could see at once that someone had bewitched the cows. "The next time one dies," he said, "cut its heart out and put some pins into it and hang it above the fire until it burns away completely." And that is what we did. And when it finished burning there was the most terrible noise I ever heard outside the door old women screaming like mad dogs. They were trying to get in, but I had turned the key, accen i. I knew who it was at once. It was my two sisters, who were envious that I had got married to Mari, and they were getting at William because he was her cousin. They screamed until the heart had disappeared altogether, and then they were silent just as the old Doctor had said. And they'd had such a fright that they never bewitched as much as a chicken ever afterwards.'[13]

Donkeys or goats were sometimes used to prevent harm to cattle.

CYFEILIOG SUPERSTITIONS. – At two farms in Cyfeiliog a donkey is kept to prevent "the creatures" being bewitched. So many of the cattle had died that advice was sought (of John Morgan, I presume), and the tenants were recommended to obtain a young donkey which had never been shod, and let him go about with the cattle. This was done, and there have been no deaths since. My informant added that the owners think more of their donkeys than of any other animal they possess, if not indeed more than of their own children. Does this superstition prevail elsewhere?[14]

REPLIES. CYFEILIOG SUPERSTITION (Sep. 10, 1890). There is a similar superstition to the one mentioned by 'R.W.,' amongst a few farmers between the dark mountains of Yale, but they give preference to the goat instead of the donkey. They believe that this bearded quadruped can prevent cows slipping their calves, and also preserve them from different diseases and from being bewitched. The only superstition regarding the donkey was (in former years) that parents were in the habit of cutting hairs off the stripe which is across the shoulders, and placing them in small bags under their children's chins to prevent the whooping cough. Llywarch Hen.[15]

Churning is a very important operation on most farms and the stories regarding failure in producing butter are very numerous. If the wife fails to get butter after churning for some time, all the doors are locked, lest the neighbours might come in and the story might get about that the farm was bewitched.

The husband then hurries to the conjuror, who usually gives him a piece of paper to stick on a particular part of the churn-then the churning is successful. They completely failed to churn on a farm and they sent for the conjuror. He came there and turned them all out of the kitchen and put a little hot water in the churn. He then tied some coloured ribbons round the legs of the churn and then churned till the butter came. He then called them in and told them never to take the ribbons off the churn, and they were there as long as the churn lasted. In another case, an old-fashioned churn was in use and one day, despite churning for hours, no butter came. The son who happened to be at home laughed at the idea of witchcraft and went to a neighbouring town and bought a new churn. All in vain, no butter resulted. The conjuror was sent for. He turned the son out of the house as he had been informed he was an unbeliever, and then emptied the churn. He then did something inside the churn, murmuring some words in doing so. He then got some fresh cream put in and butter came immediately. There was never any further trouble with churning on this farm. In another case where a conjuror was consulted about failure in churning he gave the farmer a paper, and told him to pull it over the back of the cow three times. They did so, and never had further trouble with churning.[16]

One of the last of the conjurors was Evan Griffiths, Pantybenni Llangurig area, in the old Montgomeryshire. His dates are uncertain but a photograph of him available in the People's Collection was taken in 1928.[17]

The following story was translated from a recording of the voice of the late Mr Francis Thomas, Carno.

> A farmer believed someone had put a curse on him, because his horses were dying. This is what Evan Griffiths told him to do:
> 'Go home and take the mare's heart out, and put it on a large plate in front of the fire. Right in front of the fire. And as the heart heats up, the person who has cursed you will come nearer to the house.'
> And if you know Plas Pennant, the house lies across the road, and there is a gate across the top of the farmyard, and at the bottom of the yard there is a gate leading out to the road. And he looked out of the window, and damn it, straight away this Dot from Ceulan came down past the gate. She walks past it, and past it again, just as the heart was getting hotter. And then, at last, she ventures through the gate and half way up the yard. And the old farmer said:
> 'Good God!' he said like that. 'Take the heart away! I don't want to see the devil inside this house!'[18]

Mary Lewes wrote a series of articles on weird happenings in Wales for *The Occult Review*, which were collected as *The Queer Side of Things*. Initially published in 1913, this account shows that witchcraft was still being blamed for problems with churning butter into the twentieth century, but that rational explanations were starting to supplant supernatural explanations.

> In Cardiganshire, as in many other rural districts, it was always firmly believed that when the butter would not "come" on churning-day, the cream or churn had been bewitched. There were many remedies against this trouble–one being a branch of the rowan tree hung over the dairy door; another was a knife put into the churn,

for all witches, like fairies, hate iron.

I know a house where, some few years ago, the dairymaid left in a fit of temper. Never had there been any trouble over the churning in that particularly well-regulated dairy, but, strange to say, from the week when 'Jane' left the place the butter refused to 'come.'

Churning, which in spring began early in the morning, went on for hours, everyone in the house taking a turn at the handle, and at length, towards afternoon, the long-delayed butter appeared. But what butter! It was scarcely fit to eat, and this state of things continued for several weeks, no theory of temperature, unsteady churning, or any other reason that scientific butter-makers appreciate, accounting for the extraordinary behaviour of the cream. Of course, all the local people said that Jane departing had bewitched the churn; how that was I do not know, but there is no doubt that after five or six weeks, and quite without apparent cause, the butter suddenly 'came' properly again, the 'spell' being presumably ended.[19]

I had researched and compiled the above examples and was quite happy with the results when I found myself looking at the circular symbol reproduced from Llyfr Cyfrin as a possible cover image. I knew it resembled other symbols of protection but I suddenly realised that it was more relevant than I thought. That very symbol had been used in the cattle healing charms.

Similar symbols are found in the grimoire *The Key of Solomon*. Figures with six spokes adorned with a variety of sigils are included as pentacles of various planets, some of which offer protection. The symbol itself is found in Reginald Scot's *Discoverie of Witchcraft*. This was a volume published originally in 1584 which was intended as an anti-witchcraft tract. It had a second edition in 1665, with further rituals being added. Scot was not only opposed to witchcraft and magical practice, he believed it was useless. Ironically his book became prized not for its polemic but for its inclusion of rare and valuable material, and it became a source of charms and rituals for cunning folk. Perhaps the prestige of the printed book encouraged the dynion hysbys to use the symbol from the *Discoverie of Witchcraft*, which was a rare book and not reprinted until the late twentieth century, instead of their older charms.

The symbol is printed as part of a pair in Book 15 chapter 7 with the caption, 'Who so beareth this sign about him, let him fear no foe, but fear God.'

The adjoining sign, to the left of this has the caption 'Who so beareth this signabout him, all spirits shall do him homage.'[20]

The same symbol has been found elsewhere in Wales, including in a notable charm found in Montgomeryshire. I had seen these charms previously, and even retweeted them on Twitter, without realising that the symbol was identical, give or take a little distortion in the drawing.

It might not seem unreasonable to suppose that, as we know that the symbol was used in written charms deposited in significant places in farms in the broader area, and the symbol is found in the Llyfr Cyfrin, and the author describes himself as curing cattle or helping the milk to churn, that the author used the very same charm as part of the process. It might also be reasonable to suppose that the charms found in Montgomeryshire were, if not written by the author of Llyfr Cyfrin, then were part of a continuity that included our dyn hysbys.When I was consulting Llyfr Dewiniaeth, the manuscript at the National Library of Wales which contains the seven sisters spell and other material, I also took photographs of some scraps of paper bound into the main manuscript. These are described in the National Library of Wales catalogue as 'also three charms in other hands which have been bound into the volume.'

When I transcribed these I found that they all had variations on the same charm.

The charms are all variations on a basic structure,

beseeching to Jesus Christ to preserve cow and cows and milk and cream and cheese and butter from evil humans and spirits. The list of names derives from Scot's *Discoverie of Witchcraft* where it is used for a charm against the falling sickness. After another charm 'Against the biting of a Mad Dog' a few pages later it is added, 'But where he saith, that the same hanged at a mans gate or entrie, preserveth him and his cattell from inchantment, or bewitching, he is overtaken with follie.'

This may have suggested to a cunning man that other spells in Scot's *Discoverie* may also be repurposed by hanging at a gateway to preserve cattle from witchcraft.

Whenever a cross appears the practioner was intended to cross herself if the charm was being performed aloud.

For instance,

> O Lord Jesus Christ I beseech Thee preserve cows and cow and milk and cream and cheese and butter of me? A from the power of all evil + men + women + or spirits + and from all hardness of heart + and thist I trust thou wilt do by the same power thou didst cause the blind to see the lame to walk and those that were possessed with un-clean spirit + to be in their own mind amen sweet beloved amen, pater pater pater Nos Nostera Nostera Ave ave ave Jesus Christ messiah pater et Emannuel Sabaoth Adonai imiplera ? et ma virter? para cletas salavator Noster spiritus longi?–agios adonator Jasper + Melchior + Balthasar + Matthaiso? +

(over page)

> Markus + Lucas + Johannem + that is the signs of the cross to defend his cows and milk and cream and cheese from all present past and to come inward and outward Amen Amen Amen -

More somewhat garbled Latin follows. The names Jasper + Melchior + Balthasar are those of the three magi who attended Jesus as an infant. Alexander Cummins offers several charms and more involved rituals in his *Book of the Three Magi*, along with historical analysis.

This sequence of divine names followed by the three magi and the four evangelists is found elsewhere, and clearly originates in Scot's *Discoverie of Witchcraft*. Another charm has a fuller selection of the Latin divine names.

> + Jesus + Christus + Messias + Soter + Emmanuel + Sabbaoth + Adonai + Unigenitus + Majestas + Paracletus + Salvator noster + Agiros iskiros + Agios + Adanatos + Gasper + Melchior + Balthasar + Matthaeus + Marcus + Lucas + Johannes.[21]

The memory of the image of the Montgomeryshire cattle charm was nagging at me. I started searching my hard drive for a photo of the Montgomeryshire charm that had been posted recently on Twitter. I remembered that I had reposted it myself from my @welshmyth twitter account! The photo had been posted by journalist Oli Foster, great-grandson of the man who had discovered it. I contacted Oli who told me that the charm was still in the family and was a cherished heirloom. He gave me permission to reproduce the charm and sent me an article written by his grandfather, R.H. Lloyd, the son of the farm owner who discovered it.

Lloyd wrote,

> The bottle had been broken when the stone slab above it was smashed, and he noticed that inside the bottle was a piece of paper, covered on one side with handwriting in ink, curiously cramped and closely written. At the bottom of the sheet were strange hieroglyphs, with an abracadabra triangle on the left, and a mysterious circular figure, also in ink, on the right.My father showed the paper to his parents who instantly recognised it as a conjuror's charm, which had been buried to protect the farm against witchcraft and they recalled strange happenings

which had occurred many years before in the districts of Llanfechain and Llanfyllin situated in the mountains above Welshpool.[22]

The full text of the charm was quite close to those held in the National Library.

> In the name of the Father and of the Son and of the Holy Ghost Amen xxxxx
> and in the name of the Lord Jesus Christ his redeemer and saviour he will releve
> William
> Pentrynant his cows calves
> milk butter cattle of all ages mares
> suckers horses of all ages sheep yews
> lambs sheep of all ages piges sows and
> prosper him in all his farm and from all witchcraft and all Evil diseases amen xxx
> Gasper fert Myrham thus melchor balthasar auraum hec tria quregum salvatir a morbo a Christ pretate ea duco amen xxx ineducto unversanilam amathuram positis sarah adverus artedovalis amen xxx Eructavit cor meaum verbum bonum dicam cuncta opera meregi domino labia mea aperies and os meum annutiabit vertatem cuntre brachna iniguet lingua malusgua subvertatur a Lord Jesus Christ homnorum he heareth the preserver of William Pentrynant his cows calves milk butter cattle of all ages mares suckers horses of all ages yews lambs sheep of all ages pigs sows and prosper him on this farm to live luckily saved from all witchcraft and evil men or women or spirits or wizards or hardness of heart amen xxx and this I will trust in the Lord Jesus Christ my redeemer and saviour from witchcraft amen xxx and this I trust in Jesus Christ my redeemer and saviour he will relieve William Pentrynant his calves milk butter cattle of all ages mares suckers horses of all ages yews lambs sheep of all ages pigs sows and everything (that) is his possesion to live lucken and prosper him on this farm and from all witchcraft by the same power as he did cause the blind to see the lame to walk and the dumb to

O Lord Jesus Christ I Beseech thee preserve Cows and Cow and Milk and cream and cheese and butter of me from the power of all evil & Men & Women & or spirits and from all hardness of heart & and this I trust thou wilt do by the same power thou didst cause the blind to see the lame to walk and those that were possessed with un clean spirits & to be in their own mind Amen sweet Beloved Amen pater pater pater No Nostra Pro terra Ave Ave Ave Jesus Christ & Messiah pater et Emanuel Sabaoth Adon uniplero et Majister vara cletus salavator Noster spiritus longi — agios Adonatos Jasper & Melchior & Balthasar & Mathaio & erectavit cor meum vert a cuita cor dicam louita opena mea reg Domine fe— t labia mea —osai os meum amum trahit —eritatem con terra prachia in — eam et lingua Maligna uba veritatur 1D A—

Markus & Lucas & Johanem & that is the sign of the Cross to Defend his Cows and Milk and cream and cheese from all present past and to come Inward and outward Amen Amen Amen —avit cor meum verta cor dicam ocuta ope— mea regi Domine lapia mea —perosai os meum amam trahit veritatem —terra prachia in jurean et lingua Maligna cuba vertatur —

O lou J. I beseech thee preserve & Cow and Cows and Milk and cream and cheese of me and Butter of me — from the power of all evil. & Women or spirits and from all hardness of heart and this I tru— thou wilt do by the same pow— thou didst cause the Blind to see and the lame to walk and th—

Two charms from the National Library of Wales

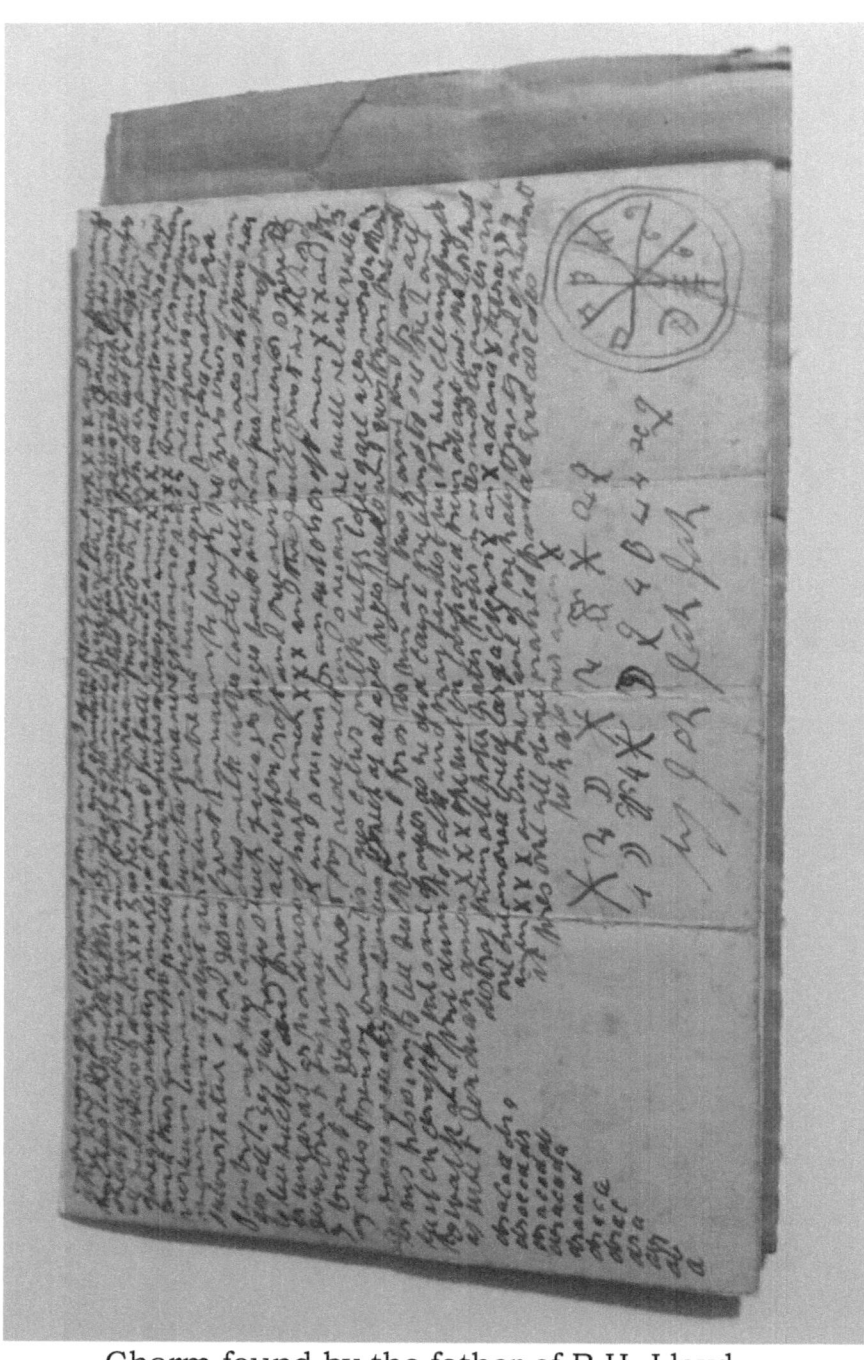

Charm found by the father of R.H. Lloyd.

talk and thou findest with unclean spirits as wilt Jehovah amen xxx the witch compassed him about but the Lord will destroy them all pater pater pater noster noster noster ave ave ave maria creed car of acteum x on x adona x tetragra amen xxx and in the name of the holy trinity and of _____ preserve all above named from all evil diseases whatsoever amen x.

Beneath two rows of astrological
signs and other hieroglyphs at the bottom of
the sheet is written: 'by Jah Jah Jah'.[23]

Lloyd explained,

the local conjuror or wise man was summoned, and he would go round the boundaries of the farm reciting his spells. This he did once on the first day, twice on the second and so on, until the seventh day, when he repeated his protective magic seven times. He then buried two written charms, one on the land itself, and one in the buildings of the farm.

It might not seem unreasonable to suppose that, as we know that the symbol was used in written charms deposited in significant places in farms in the broader area, and the symbol is found in the Llyfr Cyfrin, and the author describes himself as curing cattle or helping the milk to churn, that the author used the very same charm as part of the process. It might also be reasonable to suppose that while the charms found in Montgomeryshire were not written by the author of Llyfr Cyfrin, they were part of a continuity that included our dyn hysbys.

Notes

1 R.H. Lloyd, typescript draft of 'A Charm against Witchcraft']
2 Recounted in *Cursed Britain* p.16.
3 Elias Owen p. 230.
4 Edward Hamer and H.W. Lloyd *The History of the Parish of Llangurig* (London:1875) p. 114-115.
5 Elias Owen p. 246.
6 R. M. Evans, N.D.D., 'Folklore and Customs in Cardiganshire' Ffynnonfair, Lampeter. p.57-8
Transactions and archaeological record, Cardiganshire Antiquarian Society
https://journals.library.wales/view/1177372/1178863/58.
7 Idries Shah, *The Exploits of the Incomparable Mulla Nasrudin* p. 4 (Octagon, 1983.)
8 Elias Owen p. 238-239.
9 124 *Bye-Gones*. July 3, 1895.
https://journals.library.wales/view/2092910/2098273/#?xywh=-81%2C412%2C2910%2C1919
10 Iorwerth C. Peate, 'Welsh Folk Culture', *Welsh Outlook* Vol 19 no 11 p.296
https://journals.library.wales/view/1311205/1318758/11
11 Elias Owen p. 270-271. Owen goes on to give two short charms
ANOTHER CATTLE CHARM SPELL.
Mr. Hughes, Plasnewydd, Llansilin, lost several head of cattle. He was told to bleed one of the herd, boil the blood, and take it to the cowhouse at midnight. He did so, and lost no more after applying this charm.
A CHARM FOR CALVES.
If calves were scoured over much, and in danger of dying, a hazel twig the length of the calf was twisted round the neck like a collar, and it was supposed to cure them.
12 'The Conjuror in Montgomeryshire' p. 158-160
13 https://journals.library.wales/view/1165908/1167143/64#?xywh=-971%2C-126%2C4310%2C2843
Dillwyn Miles, 'The Last of the Traditional Storytellers 1851-1930' *Journal of the Pembrokeshire Historical Society* Vol 13 p. 57-66.
14 448 *Bye-Gones*. Sep. 10, 1890
https://journals.library.wales/view/2092910/2096866
15 492 *Bye-Gones*. Oct. 15, 1890.

https://journals.library.wales/view/2092910/2096904/15
16 Ibid. 163-164.
17 https://www.peoplescollection.wales/items/13179
18 Translation of the Welsh audio recording, https://www.peoplescollection.wales/items/606781
19 Lewes *The Queer Side of Things* p.149-150. http://gaslight-lit.s3-website.ca-central-1.amazonaws.com/gaslight/wizwales.htm
20 Reginald Scot, *Discoverie of Witchcraft* Book XV Chapter VII http://www.esotericarchives.com/solomon/scot16.htm#chap7. Interestingly, the symbol is found just before a fairy magic spell that invokes Sibylla, and another that appeals to Milia, Achilia and Sibyllia, named as three fairy sisters, who will provide the magician with a ring of invisibility. I later realised that Suggett had already realised the origin of the six-spoked symbol in A History of Magic and Witchcraft in Wales p;. 111, although he had not recognised that the appeal to the names of God, the magi and the evangelists also came from Scot.
21 *Discoverie of Witchcraft* pdf p. 186-188 cited in Alexander Cummins *A Book of the Magi: Lore, Prayers, and Spellcraft of the Three Holy Kings* (Revelore Press, 2018) p. 76. One of the charms is for "me Rolant Pugh"
22 R.H. Lloyd, typescript draft of 'A Charm against Witchcraft']
23 Spelling of the English corrected, Latin as is.

Evan Isaac also gives examples of cattle charms in his 1938 book *Coelion Cymru* p. 148-157.
Earlier examples of cattle protection charms have been published by Katherine Leach in her 2020 doctoral dissertation for Harvard University, *Healing Charms and Ritual Protection in Premodern Wales*.

Geomancy in Llyfr Cyfrin

Geomancy is a method of divination that was extremely popular in the middle ages, had a revival in the late eighteenth and early-nineteenth centuries in Europe, retains a small but active role in modern western occultism and is still a genuinely popular practice in many Arab countries. The method is essentially binary. Broken or uninterrupted lines are made from odd or even numbers of marks on earth or on a piece of paper or some other method and are combined into sets of four to produce sixteen possible types of geomantic figures. These have the Latin names Fortuna Major, Fortuna Minor, Via, Populus, Acquisitio, Laetitia, Puella, Amissio, Conjunctio, Albus, Puer, Rubeus, Carcer, Tristitia, Caput Draconis, Cauda Draconis.

These figures may be favourable or unfavourable and have the seven classical planets and nodes of the moon assigned to them.

Kate Bosse-Griffiths has a short section on the geomancy contained in Llyfr Cyfrin.

On several non-consecutive pages (p. 1, 2, 20-1, 137-9, 145-6 and on some unnumbered pages) the Dyn Hysbys recorded a geomantic method which enabled him to read a fortune with the co-operation of the questioner.

The principle of the arrangement is simpler than playing cards, and it would be easy to practice it to entertain friends. The success of the exercise depends on the degree to which the magician is able to reach the subconscious of the questioner.[1]

These pages contain a 'method' rather than the geomantic workings of the dyn hysbys. Bosse-Griffiths continues,

> To create the proper atmosphere the Dyn Hysbys would begin with a 'Prayer of Geomancy' begging God to make 'this said figure of geomancy' in order to come up with a true and perfect answer, in the name of Jesus Christ, our Lord and Saviour.

Although she does not give the prayer, it may be found in a popular book of the time, *The Universal Fortune-teller* by John Parkins. The prayer matches that given by Bosse-Griffiths, as it also contains the phrase, 'this said figure of geomancy' and ends 'for the sake of Jesus Christ our Lord and Saviour, Amen.' The book was published in 1810. Adverts for books of fortune telling and occult lore appeared in the *North Wales Gazette* at least from 1811 to 1825, with *The Universal Fortune-teller* often received star billing in the ads, so it was clearly available to the compiler of Llyfr Cyfrin.

The full prayer given on p. 71 is as follows,

> O Almighty and most merciful Lord God, I thy poor humble unworthy servant do now most humbly beseech and entreat thee, That thou wilt, of thy great mercy and goodness, so guide, direct, and govern my soul, my guardian angel, and also my hand, in the making and forming of this said figure of Geomancy; that I may now immediately obtain a most true and perfect answer unto to this question, which I now propound unto thee, in the due and proper means which thou hast been most graciously pleased to bestow, and give unto me, for the sake of Jesus Christ our Lord and Saviour, Amen.[2]

She goes on,

The questioner is then directed to quickly make four lines of dots regardless of the number. When judging the dots, the only thing that matters is whether or not the number is even (a multiple of two). To compose the geomantic figure, one point is set down for each odd line and two points for each even line. Using four line figures it is possible to get sixteen variations, and therefore the same number of different geomantic figures. Each of the figures is given a Latin name and is linked in twos to the "planets" who rule the week. namely the Sun (Sunday), the Moon (Monday), Mars (Tuesday), Mercury (Wednesday), Jupiter (Thursday) Venus (Friday). Saturn (Saturday) – and the dragon. As we are familiar with the practice of associating the planets with particular aspects – Mars with war, Venus with love and so on – it would be possible to guess answers from the above list only.'

The material in the notebook is in English but she has translated it into Welsh. Unfortunately she doesn't give us the page numbers in Llyfr Cyfrin in which she found the material.

Her table of geomantic figures derives from p. 480-485, but it she has listed the interpretations under the name of each figure, in order from Fortuna Major to the Dragon's Tail rather than the order of *The Familiar Astrologer*, by 'oracle', giving the visual figure itself without the figure name. It seems likely that this is a product of Bosse-Griffiths digesting and reorganising the material in Llyfr Cyfrin in order to present it to her audience, rather than the author of Llyfr Cyfrin changing the order when he transcribed the material from *The Familiar Astrologer*.

There were other surces of geomantic material available by the time of the Llyfr Cyfrin. In 1830 Robert Roberts published *Seryddiaeth*, a compendium of magic and divination in Welsh which gave the basics of geomancy plus extensive interpretations of the associations between the geomantic figures and the astrological houses. The geomantic material included a Welsh translation of the Geomancy sections in the *Fourth Book of Occult Philosophy* compilation.

Another immediate possible source could be *The Familiar Astrologer*, from which the Llyfr Cyfrin compiler has taken some spells. This has sections on geomancy beginning on pages 28-32, 103-113, 176-187, 349-357, 457-465, 480-485 ('Secrets of Geomancy Translated from Peruchio'), 643-651, 661-665 ('The Oracle of Dreams According to the Earl of Essex' Manuscript')

And indeed the section titled 'The Oracle of Dreams' used geomancy as a method of interpreting dreams, referring to the querent as the dreamer, matching Kate Bosse-Griffiths' description.[3]

The Oracle of Dreams in *The Familiar Astrologer* is extracted, Robert Cross Smith tells us, from a manuscript the entirety of which was published in 1834 as *The Royal Book of Fate From an Illuminated Manuscript, Found in the Library of the Unfortunate Earl of Essex, who was Beheaded in the Reign of Queen Elizabeth: a Work of the Greatest Interest, Curious, Marvellous, and Wonderful, Relating to Love, Marriage, Riches, Dreams Foretold, and All Subjects of Fate, Chance, and Mortal Destiny.*

His earlier *The Philosophical Merlin*, which also contained a system of geomancy, claimed to have been formerly in the possession of Napoleon Buoneparte.

Bosse-Griffiths goes on to give the shortest examples she can in Llyfr Cyfrin of the meaning of the geomantic figures. While it is understandable that, in writing a book in Welsh about a Welsh subject, she wished to limit the quotation of English-language material, it was a little frustrating that she doesn't quote the geomantic material directly but translates it into Welsh.

1. Fortuna. Very lucky in gold and silver and the best of goods, perhaps an unexpected gift from friends.
2 Fortuna Minor. Money, friends and an agreeable fate.

3. Via. This predicts misfortune that is difficult to avoid; it also means personal enemies.

4 Populus. The dream is mainly news related. The absent will come back; expresses the sign of relative fortune and good luck; also, often traveling near water.

5 Acquisitio. This shows invitations, gifts and changing the present situation to advantage.

6 Laetitia. This dream is happy and fulfilling. It means favourable meeting and feasting, and good news is near.

7 Puella. Getting married if single, and children if married. Success in most things.

8 Amissa. You must beware of some untrustworthy person close to the querent: perhaps some loss.

9 Conjunctio. This involves dealing with papers, charts, books and written matters for various purposes.

10 Albus. A good sign. The dreamer will achieve his will but often buries a friend.

11 Puer. Nasty and wild words. Fighting and trouble in the dreamer's life and destiny.

12 Rubeo. A sign of anger, terror, bad feelings and deceitful counselors. Take care!–enemies are close.

13 Carcer. Take care lest your enemy hurt you; maybe something in connection with prison. This sign also speaks of sad distress.

14 Tristitia. This signifies misfortune and sorrow, and it is possible that friends will die.

15 The Dragon's Head. A successful and lucky fortune with some sort of prospect to be expected. A journey will follow.

16 The Dragon's Tail. If this has any significance, it signifies something bad.

The short discussion of geomancy ends with a paragraph on contemporary Geomancy in Nigeria and a translation into Welsh of a Nigerian *odu* verse that offered geomantic interpretation.

From the limited evidence supplied by Kate Bosse-Griffiths we may conclude that the the compiler of Llyfr Cyfrin included geomantic material that was available in *The Universal Fortune-teller* and *The Familiar Astrol-*

oger, and possibly other publications. Geomancy was newly fashionable again in in Britain and the inclusion of these sections in Llyfr Cyfrin reflects the mixture of traditional methods and book research typical of cunning folk. The lack of geomantic workings in the notebook does not mean that the dyn hysbys never attempted geomantic divination. *The Familiar Astrologer* suggests 'marking down with pen, pencil, or any other instrument, upon paper, slate, or any other legible material, a certain number of points, leaving the precise number to chance. . .'[4]

The impermanent horary nature of geomantic workings and the necessity of working out the mothers, daughters, nephews, witnesses and judge from the initial figure commended itself to the use of reusable or cheap materials. Chalk markings on slate which was later wiped clean would have been ideal, especially as slate was so easily available in north Wales.

Notes

1 *The Universal Fortune-teller* p. 71. Kate Bosse-Griffiths doesn't cite any printed work on geomancy in her bibliography.
2 The geomancy section is found on p. 46-50 of *Byd y Dyn Hysbys*. All translations are my own.
3 Much of the most interesting material from the book of Robert Cross Smith ('Raphael') may be found in the compilation edited by John Madziarczyk, *A Sorcerous Anthology:Magical and Occult Writings from the Publications of Robert Cross Smith* (Topaz House Publications, 2017).
4 *The Familiar Astrologer* p. 105; *A Sorcerous Anthology* p. 53.

Appendices

Dewinesau Dinbych

The Witches of Denbigh

The story of the witch of Endor is to be found in the Bible. Is it only to women that this witchcraft[1] belongs? We find that Twm o'r Nant understands it better than many. He mentions them in his interludes, and if necessary he could play a wizard-like role himself. It is said that a hideous spirit disturbed a family in Bryn Lluarth, a place about three miles from Denbigh. It knocked on the doors, threw soot in the soup, watered the milk, broke the dishes, and enacted various other dirty tricks. To get rid of it there was nothing to do but get Twm o'r Nant to put it down. After being hired, Twm started to do his work, and he was at it for three days and three nights. The great challenge, despite how much he read out aloud to it, was to bring the spirit to visible appearance. It came to appearance in the end in the form of an elephant, and Twm read on until it became a small bull, then a wolf, a mad dog, a vicious cat, a rat, a weasel, and finally a dead fly.[2] After becoming so small, despite all its screams, Twm was able to get it into his tobacco box; and he buried it in a marsh nearby, never to trouble anyone while there was running water. If Tom was able to play tricks like these, it was not odd that he was so fond of mentioning them in his interludes.

In the interlude 'Pleser a Gofid' Twm showed that he was familiar with the art of telling fortunes. He includes the names of books related to the art, such as 'Hocus Pocus,' 'Wheel of Fortune,' 'Book of Knowledge,' and 'Cornelius Agrippa.' Twm includes Sal o'r South as a character who tells fortunes, and Rondol the miser goes to her to receive knowledge of his destiny. At his entrance Sal o'r South greets him courteously:-

> By your leave, my master
> I bow to you.

But Rondol has a dry enough reply, 'I would rather not give a kick to your fashion.'

When Sal tells his fortune to him in the following words,

> ' know by the book the luck that follows
> The size of the planet explains your fortune.
> You will get plenty of money with the fairness of dawn
> And great happiness from your smallholding.

Rondol is so pleased that he breaks out in the following words,

> We talk about some vain rubbish,
> Sian and Sioned, and Rebela from Denbigh,
> They're, not fit to open their mouth,
> They are not from the South but are dross.

The Rebela mentioned in the above verse was Bela Fawr from Denbigh. A woman stout of body was Bela, making some understand that she was a second Mary Magdalene. Bela's main function was to handle the spirits that troubled the country. It was assumed that she was capable of putting them down like Twm o'r Nant. A question may be asked about stories like this,—were those that were causing trouble at that time under the authority of the evil one, or were they tricks caused by neighbours? I heard the following anecdote from someone I trust. Two strangers once came to Rhyl. After lodging in a house for some time, the woman of the house charged an exorbitant price for their room. They paid her in a grudging manner, and went away. After a short time the tea service in the cupboard started to shake and continued to do so from time to time until the cupboard had to be taken down, and they found a piece of paper pushed under the cupboard; no one could read it. After burning it in the fire and putting the cupboard in its place, nothing moved after that.

Someone is said to have come to Bela once, complaining that something was troubling his house. Following the man was a huge dog. After sending his message to Bela, Bela asked him if he would like to see the spirit, and she called for someone to come from the back, dressed as a ghost–if a ghost has clothes. When the dog saw such an ugly creature, he jumped at her with his teeth, and Bela had to persuade the man to take away his dog, and it was clearly seen that a man from the town was playing the part of the spirit for Bela. There was not much lustre to Bela's claims after this time.

There was another living around the same time as Bela, Elen Ann Pughe.

Elen did not claim to be able to handle spirits. Her path was more concerned with the world of romance. At night she was able to do her work. Many single people approached her, men and women, to try to find out each other's history from her. She claimed to be able to interpret mysteries in the business of love, and it is very easy in every age to find customers who have a deep desire to know each other's past. Nel's sun went down like Bela's, and they were replaced by a brighter sun in the person of one named Miss Lloyd.

Miss Lloyd was the daughter of a clergyman, and despite all her ability to see into the future as a diviner [dewines], she could not foresee her own dilemma. She fell in love with a young gentleman, and the love affair went on for some time. But when he was about to go and marry her, the young man's wife came into sight, and the young man ran away, and was never seen again. But as each time a bad turn or a good turn happens, a second and a third come. Shortly after this, Miss Lloyd's father died, leaving her without a penny in her possession. She now had to face the world alone. She was well educated, and probably had an inclination towards the art of fortune-telling. She bought Sydney Talbot's 'Book of Fate' and other books. Very soon she came to be doing a roaring trade with the art. While engaged in this work she lived in Park Lane, opposite the then public house, known as the 'Union.' She was a strange creature, seeming to have been in continual communion with unearthly beings. In the kitchen she had a squirrel and a guinea pig running around. When someone came to the house, these creatures entertained themselves by making the loudest noise, to reassure customers that their mistress was having contact with someone who was helping her in the art. Her house was not a pleasant place to visit and no one approached her except those who were in trouble. The sight of her doing her work made many believe she had a close friendship with Old Nick. In the time of Miss Lloyd the policemen were very incompetent in their work, with not much of the detective's art; so she was a great asset for catching thieves, and for bringing to light those who took other people's things, but unfortunately forgot to bring them back. It is very difficult for some in this age to believe the following anecdotes, but they are perfectly true. I was listening to a relative tell one story, and since I was not quite ready to believe in Miss Lloyd's ability, I cross-examined him in great detail, and was surprised that I had been doubting what was perfectly true.

   A merchant from this town lost a piece of cloth from his bakery, and happened to tell Edwin, Miss Lloyd's son, who, without losing any time, said, 'Go home to check with your mam, that you are sure of this.' Before dark that night, a woman came back with the piece of cloth, saying that it had been taken by mistake. Another person in the town had lost a piece of bacon, and could not know who had taken it: and with more curiosity than any other, he approached Miss Lloyd, and she told him, 'He will come to meet you in Park Lane very soon with a pickaxe and shovel on his back.' And he came, and the owner of the bacon explained to him when and how the bacon was taken.

In a grand house on Vale Street a lawyer's wife had lost her gold spectacles, and because she was one of those who knocked back a drop after lunch, making her feel drowsy and sleepy, and arousing in her a weary feeling, it was as if she reached out to the maids about her glasses. One evening the two maids decided to go to Miss Lloyd, they were willing to pay ninepence each for a hint about the spectacles and to get some peace. In the darkness they ran to Miss Lloyd's house, her house was only fifty yards away. When they knocked on the door they went in, and the first thing Miss Lloyd told them was, 'You have lost something.' When they both answered, she said again, 'You will find them locked up in one of the upper rooms of the house.' When the subject of the spectacles came up the next day, it wasn't long before they led their mistress to go and look at some a box she had in her bedroom, and there they were.

Some would come to Miss Lloyd not only from the town but from far afield. A lady in Ruthin had lost a silk cloth, and as she was unsure who had taken it, she approached Miss Lloyd. After Miss Lloyd had gone through her routines, she took her to a back room and showed the woman the person who had taken it standing behind her in the mirror, and told her, 'The woman who stole it lives over the water—the river Llanfwrog—and she will bring the cloth back to you. 'And so the woman brought it back to her.

Many at that time thought that Miss Lloyd could explain all mysteries, even if some sickness might bother them. Something had come to annoy a respectable and responsible man in this town, until he eventually had to be sent to the asylum. No one knew what was annoying him. To find out the mystery went to Miss Lloyd; but the only answer she gave was that he would come to himself, and that he would be home soon. The man came as she said, but he never was the same again.

A man in the parish of Llanrhaiadr had lost a piece of beef, and in order to know who the thief was, he approached Miss Lloyd. After telling her the message, she asked him if he would allow her to make a mark of the beef on his face, probably as an image of the piece of beef. It is not stated so, but it is likely that the man allowed her to do such a thing. At least he said nothing to the contrary. When he paid her, the man went home, and within a few days saw a neighbour with a mark on his face of the same image of the beef. The owner was surprised when he saw who had taken the beef. The mark was on the man as long as he lived.

A woman had once lost rent money from her house. She went to tell Miss Lloyd her problem, and Miss Lloyd gave her a description of the woman who took the money. Miss Lloyd said to her, 'The woman and the money will come back to you, and the dress she is wearing will be such-and-such.' And the thief brought back the money as Miss Lloyd said.

It is said that Miss Lloyd did not fail to come true with her claims. If divination can be called an art, Miss Lloyd had learned it thoroughly. She didn't fail to please anyone who came to her. Miss Lloyd was quite fond of a drop, and one night she went to Edwin Hughes' vaults to ask for a shilling of liquor, and she said to the barman, 'I never had such a job to come up the alley as tonight.' 'What's the matter, Miss Lloyd?' he said. 'Well,' she said, 'they were around me like bees tonight; I would for the life of me ignore them.' Having got the liqueur, she went home talking loudly to herself the whole way.

She died at the bottom of Henllan Street at a considerable age, and is said to have looked awful at the end of her life.

'Dewinesau Dinbych' *Cymru* 30: 127–29.

Endnotes

1 Swyngyfaredd.
2 Probably a reference to Ecclesiastes 10:1 'Gwybêd meirw a ddrwant,' 'Dead flies cause the ointment of the apothecary to send forth a stinking savour: so doth a little folly him that is in reputation for wisdom and honour.'

Welsh Astrologers, Sorcerers, &C-

There were several persons in North Wales about the first quarter of the present century pretending to be astrologers and to practise sortilege. Among the most noted were Mochyn Nant (Pig of the Dingle), John Evans, keeper of Elian's Well, Shon Rhosesmor, Bella, Sionet Gorn, and Sydney of Denbigh, Mary the White Mantle, and Shon Gyfarwydd of Llanbrynmair. These persons were very cunning in their dealings, and often eluded the vigilance of the law. They were mostly supported by the farmers, and the ignorant amongst the masses of the people, who consulted them continually respecting thefts, curses, and local occurrences difficult to comprehend. Their answers and advice in some cases proved successful and beneficial to themselves, owing to their shrewdness and craft in dealing with people's weaknesses and simplicity. But they often made mistakes, and were liable to be detected by the skilful and the ingenious, as in the case of Mochyn Nant, who was lashed and held up to ridicule by Jonathan Hughes, the bard, and Thomas De Quincey. It appears by the poet's song that a fat sheep, intended to be slaughtered against Nerquis Wakes, was stolen from one William Williams, and was found some weeks afterwards strangled in a building amongst some loose straw. Williams, foolishly enough, went over the mountains to Penycae, Ruabon, to consult Mochyn Nant regarding the occurrence:–

I dystio ei destyn wrth Fochyn y Nant,

Mochyn Nant gave him a paper to put under his head, telling him that the consequence would be that he would see the thief in a dream:–

Cewchweled wynebryd
Y lleidr mewn breuddwyd.

The Mochyn promised Williams in a second journey to show the thief's face in a glass, and also to place a mark on his nose:–

I'r lleidryn tywyllodrus yn gymwys tan go,
Cael mark a ddewisai lle fynai arno fo;
Ar y llwdwn bras aden
'Roedd pitch yn llythyren;
A dyna'r nod enwog ddewisai'r perchenog,
Ar drwyn y gŵr chwanog fu lwynog rhy flin.

But, said Mochyn suddenly, 'You had better go home, and put this paper in the soil of his garden, and the thief will never be at ease':–

Ni chaiff ef byth wed'yn esmwythder fynudyn,
Bydd draen yn ei drwynyn yr hurtyn anhardd.

In the year 1802, when De Quincey was staying at Ruabon, during the philosopher's wanderings in Wales, he paid a visit to Mochyn Nant, accompanied by a female friend, who presented him to the great interpreter of the stars in person. He was 'anxious to make the acquaintance of an astrologer, and especially of one who, whilst owning to so rare a profession, owned also to the soft impeachment of so very significant a name.' About Mochyn's dress, the writer remarks, 'there was a forlornness and an ancient tarnish or aerugo, which went far to justify the name; and upon his face there sat that lugubrious rust which medallists technically call patina. . . . Speaking humanly one would have insinuated that the star-gazer wanted much washing and scouring; but, astrologically speaking, perhaps he would have been spoiled by earthly waters for his celestial vigils.' The essayist describes the different processes the great astrologer went through in reading his destinies, how he went into an adjoining room to construct his horoscope, remaining there for half an hour drinking bottled porter, and how he returned with a folio book under his arm, said to be a manuscript of great antiquity, looking more lugubrious than ever–more grim, more rusty and more in want of scouring. Also how he read with a steady Pythian fury in a dreadful voice the dreadful starry charges against the philosopher, and the things that he was to do, and the things that he was not to do. Moreover the writer on walking to the table where the astrologer sat, in order to pay his fees, came nearer to the folio book which was spread open than astrological prudence would have allowed, when the Pig's attention was diverted with the silver coins, and saw at a glance that it was no MS., but a printed book in black-letter type. De Quincey shook hands and exchanged kind farewells with Mochyn Nant, who smiled benignly upon him in total forgetfulness that he had just dismissed the philosopher to a life of storms, and so De Quincey quitted the Dingle for ever, thus ending his first and last visit to an astrologer. As far as I can remember the Pig of the Dingle died about 32 years ago, and was interred at Ruabon.

Ffynnon Elian, or the Cursing Well, is situated in the township of Eirias, in the parish of Llandrillo-yn-Rhos. This noted well had great influence for generations, until some years ago. Ignorant and superstitious people were in the habit of visiting the place by hundreds from all parts of North Wales, and the owner of the well made a lucrative business. The usual way of cursing was for the applicant to stand upon a certain spot near the well, whilst the keeper read some portions of Scripture, and afterwards gave some of the water to the former to drink, throwing the remainder over his head, which was repeated three times, the keeper muttering curses during the process. At the Ruthin Assizes, held Aug. 3, 1831, before Judge Bolland, one John Evans, a keeper of this well, was convicted and sentenced to six months' imprisonment. The prosecutrix was one Elizabeth Davies, who said in evidence that she had walked twenty-two miles to have her husband's name, who was pining away with sickness, taken out of the well, and had to pay the defendant ten shillings, it being the lowest charge. The defendant raised from the middle of the well some small square slates, having different letters on them. He gave her a slate with R.D. on it, and said it must be her husband's name, and that she was to take it home, not showing it any one, and to grind it small, mixing it with salt, and throwing it afterwards into the fire. He also gave her a bottle of water from the well, and muttered something 'in Latin,' which she could not understand, besides 'Ab Elian,' for which she had to pay nine shillings. Her husband was to take the water for three nights and to read the thirty-eighth Psalm. The defendant wanted to enter the man in the well who had put her husband there, but she would not allow him to do so; he was also very cross with Mr Clough, a Justice of the Peace. After this exposure the fame of the well soon vanished into oblivion; so the place is now seldom visited, except by the antiquary and the curious. There were other noted wells, viz., Ffynon Tegla, Llandegla, and the one at Rhosesmor, near Mold, kept by an old shoe maker, who met with a similar fate to that of the keeper of St. Elian's well, at Flint Castle. Old Bella, Sioned Corn, and Sydney were noted witches in their days, residing at Denbigh, the last in a small hut on the brink of Lenten Pool, and imposing on the credulity of the people by pretending to foretell future events with cards and other such rubbish. One night three young men called upon Sydney for their fortunes, one of them having a particular desire to see the devil, and offering a handsome fee to gratify his curiosity. Sydney, after cautioning them not to move a finger, went through some mysterious mummeries, and blew out the candle, when suddenly the rattle of chains and unearthly sounds were heard in the adjoining room. Soon through the dim light of the fire something was seen in the shape of an ox, butting the door with his horns, and stamping the threshold with his hoofs, when one of the spectators shouted,'Come forward, Satan, don't be afraid to show yourself!' The demon made a rush forward with a roar, but a large mastiff, which one of the men had brought with him, sprang in an instant at the throat of the apparition, and would have worried him sadly had he not shouted out 'murder.' The demon, after being stripped of the hide, proved to be a well known accomplice of old Sydney's whom she had trained in the business from a child. Mary Evans, or Mary the White Mantle, was a native of Cardiganshire. She lived at one time at Maentwrog, and had many disciples at Festiniog, whose religion was something similar to Johana Southcott's. Her followers, when offended, used to take held of each other's hands by the doors of their opponents' houses, and fall together on their knees uttering awful curses against their enemies. Mary was buried at Llanfihangel Traethau, where a stone is placed over her remains. The last of this race was old John Roberts, Shon Gyfarwydd, who died a few years ago at Llanbrynmair. It is surprising to learn how many people in this 'enlightened age,' who considered themselves respectable, were in the habit of consulting this oracle occasionally, respecting future events, petty larcenies, local matters, and different diseases in human beings and animals. Ignorance and superstition have not quite vanished from amongst us; they are to be seen not in the remotest regions, and not so much amongst the working classes, but amongst people thinking themselves much higher, and even wearing the cloak of religion. Llwyn Dedwydd.

Llywarch Hen

Aug. 29, 1888. BYE-GONES. 177

Further Reading

Anonymous, 'The Year's Sleep ; Or, the Forest of the Yew Tree' The Cambrian quarterly magazine and Celtic repertory No. 5 January 1 - 1830

Bain, Frederika, 'The Binding of the Fairies: Four Spells' in *Preternature: Critical and Historical Studies on the Preternatural* , no. 2 (2012) pp. 323-354.

Bosse-Griffiths, Kate, *Byd y Dyn Hysbys* (Y Lolfa, 1977)

Briggs, Katherine *Fairies in Tradition and Literature* (Routledge, 2002)

Briggs, Katharine, 'Some Seventeenth-Century Books of Magic' in *Folklore*, Vol. 64, No. 4 (Dec., 1953), pp. 445-462

Briggs, Katherine, *The Anatomy of Puck* (Routledge & Paul, 1959).

Bromwich, Rachel, *Trioedd Ynys Prydein The Triads of the Island of Britain (*4th edition, University of Wales Press, 2017).

Clark, J. Kent Clark, *Goodwin Wharton* (Penguin, 1989)..

Collins, Fiona, *Denbighshire Folk Tales* (The History Press, 2011

Adam Coward, 'Rejecting Mother's Blessing: the Absence of the Fairy in the Welsh Search for Identity' *Proceedings of the Harvard Celtic Colloquium*, Vol. 29 (2009), pp. 57-69.

Cummins, Alexander, *A Book of the Magi: Lore, Prayers, and Spellcraft of the Three Holy Kings* (Revelore Press, 2018).

Cutchin, Joshua, *A Trojan Feast* (Anomalist Books 2015).

Davies, J.H. (Penardd) 'Lloffion Llenyddol. Hen Ddewiniaid Cymru. Ellis Edwart' in *The London Kelt* 18th May 1901

D'Este, Sorita and Rankine, David (eds.) *The Faerie Queens: A Collection of Essays Exploring the Myths, Magic and Mythology of the Faerie Queens* (Avalonia, 2013).
Evans Hugh, *Y Tylwyth Teg* (Yng Ngwasg Y Brython, 1935).
Evans, Owen 'Dewinesau Dinbych' in *Cymru* vol. 30 1906 pp.127-129
Foulkes, Isaac. 'Dyffryn clwyd: ei ramantau a'i Lafar Gwlad' *Transactions of the Cymmrodorion Society* Sess. 1892-3. pp. 88-103
Fulton, Helen, *Selections From the Dafydd ap Gwilym Apocrypha* (Gomer Press, 1996)
Gerald of Wales, Lewis Thorpe (trans.) *The Journey Through Wales/The Description of Wales* (Penguin, 1978).
Griffiths, Gwyn 'Swyn i atal serch', *Heddiw* 6, 1941 pp. 177-8.
Griffiths, Gwyn 'A Modern Welsh Anti-Love Charm with Ancient Antecedents'. *Anthropos* 60, 1965 pp.108-12.
Griffiths, J. Gwyn, '"Arepo" in the Magic "Sator" Square' in *The Classical Review* Vol. 21, No. 1 (Mar., 1971), pp. 6-8 https://www.jstor.org/stable/707027
Gruffydd, Eirlys *Gwrachod Cymru* (Gwasg Gwynedd, 1980)
Gruffydd, Heini, *A Haven From Hitler* (Y Lolfa, 2014)
Harms, Daniel *Book of Oberon* (Llewellyn, *2015)*.
Harms, Daniel 'Of Fairies: An Excerpt from a Seventeenth-Century Magical Manuscript' Folklore Volume 129, 2018 - Issue 2 pp.192-198
Harms, Daniel 'Hell and Fairy: The Differentiation of Fairies and Demons Within British Ritual Magic of the Early Modern Period' in *Knowing Demons, Knowing Spirits in the Early Modern Period* (Palgrave MacMillan 2018).
Harms, Daniel *Of Angels, Demons and Spirits: A*

Sourcebook of British Magic (Llewllyn 2019).
Hartland E. Sidney 'The Treasure on the Drim,' *The Folk-Lore Journal* 1888 6:1, pp.125-128,
Hunter, Jack, 'Rev. Elias Owen and the Folklore of the Tanat Valley' https://www.academia.edu/49085497/Rev_Elias_Owen_and_the_Folklore_of_the_Tanat_Valley_Full_
Hutton, Ronald 'The Making of the Early Modern British Fairy Tradition' *The Historical Journal*, (2014). 57(4), 1157-75
Hutton, Ronald *Queens of the Wild* (Yale University Press, 2022).
Jones, Edmund *The Appearance of Evil* (University of Wales Press, 2003).
Jones, T. Gwynn *Welsh Folklore and Folk-Custom* (reprint D.S.Brewer, 1979)
Olsan, Lea T. 'Writing On The Hand in Ink: A Late Medieval Innovation in Fever Charms in England' https://www.researchgate.net/publication/332271713_Writing_on_the_Hand_in_Ink_A_Late_Medieval_Innovation_in_Fever_Charms_in_England
Jones J (Myrddin Fardd) *Llên Gwerin Sir Gaernarfon* (Gwmni y Cyhoeddwyr Cymreig, Swyddfa Cymru, 1908)
Kruse, John *Love and Sex in Faeryland* (Independently published, 2021).
Lewes, Mary, *The Queer Side of Things* 1912 Selwyn, 1923.
Lilly, William (Katherine Briggs, ed.) *The Last of the Astrologerz* (The Folklore Society, 1974)
Löffler, Marion 'Bosse-Griffiths, Kate (1910-98)' in *Celtic Culture: A Historical Encyclopedia* ed. John T. Koch
Luft D. *Medieval Welsh Medical Texts: Volume One: The Recipes* [Internet] (University of Wales Press; 2020.
Madziarczyk, John, *A Sorcerous Anthology:Magical and Occult Writings from the Publications of Robert Cross Smith* (Topaz House Publications, 2017).

Miles, Dillwyn, 'The Last of the Traditional Storytellers 1851-1930' *Journal of the Pembrokeshire Historical Society* Vol 13 p. 57-66.
Owen, Elias *Welsh Folk-lore A Collection of the Folk-Tales and Legends of North Wales*. [Online] Available from: http://www.gutenberg.org/files/20096/20096-h/20096-h.htm
Owen, Hywel Wyn and Morgan, Richard *Dictionary of the Place-Names of Wales* (Gwasg Gomer, 2008).
Owen, Morfydd E. Review of Byd y Dyn Hysbys in *Y Traethodydd* Cyf. CXXXIV, Rhif 570, Ionawr 1979 p.171-172
Evans, Owen 'Dewinesau Dinbych' *Cymru* Vol XXX, Caernarfon, 1906.
Parkin, Sally Women. Witchcraft and the Law in Early Modern Wales (1536-1736): A Continuation of Customary Practice 1998/2000/2002
Pugh, Edward, *Cambria Depicta: a Tour Through North Wales: Illustrated with Picturesque Views* (Williams, 1816).
Purkiss, Diane *Fairies and Fairy Stories: a History* (Tempus Publishing, 2008).
Rankine, David *The Book of Treasure Spirits* (Avalonia, 2009).
Raphael (David Cross Smith), *The Familiar Astrologer*, (John Bennett, 1832).
Redway, George, *The Astrologer's Guide* (George Redway, 1886)
Rudiger, Angelika *Y Tylwyth Teg. An Analysis of a Literary Motif.* https://research.bangor.ac.uk/portal/files/40328713/2021_R_diger_AH_PhD.pdf
Sikes Wirt *British Goblins* https://www.gutenberg.org/files/34704/34704-h/34704-h.htm
Simek, Rudolf 'Tangible Religion: Amulets, Illnesses, and the Demonic Seven Sisters' https://www.stockholmuniversitypress.se/site/chapters/e/10.16993/bay.m/

Stephens, Meic 'Obituary: Kate Bosse Griffiths' *Independent* Friday 10 April 1998 https://www.independent.co.uk/news/obituaries/obituary-kate-bossegriffiths-1155460.html
Suggett, Richard, *A History of Magic and Witchcraft in Wales* (The History Press, 2008).
Suggett, Richard *Welsh Witches:: Narratives of Witchcraft and Magic from sixteenth- and seventeenth-century Wales* (Atramentous Press, 2018)
T. P., (Lisa Tallis, ed.) *Cas Gan Gythraul: Demonology, Witchcraft, and Popular Magic in Eighteenth-Century Wales* (South Wales Record Society, 2015).
Tallis, Lisa Mari, 'Witches, Gypsies, and the Fenyw Hysbys in Eighteenth-Century Wales' 'preternature_8_2_231
Tallis, Lisa Mari, Welsh Witchcraft Revelations and Ruins: the Example of Mari Berllan Biter preternature_11_1_43
Thomas, W. Jenkyns *The Welsh Fairy Book*. (A. & C. Black, 1938)
Williams, John *Ancient And Modern Denbigh* (J. Williams, 1856)
Wood, Juliette 'A Fairy Bride among the Druids: Narrating Identity in a Welsh Folk Tale' https://www.academia.edu/38682854/A_Fairy_Bride_Among_the_Druids
'The Binding of the Fairies' *Preternature Critical and Historical Studies on the Preternatural* Scholarly Publishing Collective https://scholarlypublishingcollective.org/psup/preternature/article-abstract/1/2/323/290348/The-Binding-of-the-Fairies-Four-Spells
Waters, Thomas *Cursed Britain: A History of Witchcraft and Black Magic in Modern Times* (Yale University Press 2020).
Young, Simon and Houlbrook, Ceri (ed.) *Magical Folk: British and Irish Fairies* (Gibson Square, 2018)

Index

Aberbargod 110
Abercuch 110
Abergavenny 181
Aberystruth 84, 85, 91
Aberystwyth 3, 86, 87, 94, 132
abracadabra 192, 201
Abraham 128
Achilia 131, 207
Adam 142
AGLA 65, 137
Agrippa 125, 218
alchemical 60
angels 38, 48, 56, 60, 75, 89, 140, 209
apocrypha 79, 89
apparition 136, 153, 229
archangels 140
Avalonia 88, 140

bacon 148, 221
balthasar 200–202
Barampar 34, 35, 65
bard 158, 225
Bartholomew 52, 69, 73
Beckerman, Jane 154
bewitched 7, 9, 10, 112, 148, 152, 170, 176, 180–83, 185, 186, 189, 191, 195–98, 200
Bible 62, 188, 217
bleed 206
bleeding 71, 192
blind 200, 202
Bodleian 60, 61
bookbinder 171, 172, 178
Bosse-Griffiths, Kate 1–4, 6, 7, 9, 10, 12, 21, 22, 42,

43, 45–47, 50, 51, 60, 62, 64, 65, 69, 71, 74, 98, 128, 129, 133, 140, 141, 144, 162, 172, 180, 183, 208–12, 214
bottle 135, 176, 177, 192, 193, 201, 228
boundaries 31, 33, 62, 144, 205
Braich-y-Ddinas 129, 132, 141
Breconshire, Brecknockshire 77, 193
Bridgend 87
Briggs, Katherine 91, 117–19, 121, 123, 124, 131
Brychan 76–78
Bryneglwys 81, 190
Bryngarw 87
butter 10, 126, 130, 180, 185, 187–89, 193, 196–98, 200, 202
Bye-gones 163, 165, 169, 177-8, 206, 230

Cadwgan 5
Caerleon 88, 108
Caernarvonshire 168
calfskins 35, 65
Cambria 123, 143, 148-9, 156, 162-3
Capricornus 42, 69
Cardans 40, 66
Cardiff 65
Cardiganshire 63, 86, 185, 197, 206, 229
cattle 1, 7, 9, 10, 54, 74, 78, 86, 87, 90, 102, 113, 114, 148, 161, 164, 166, 168, 170, 173, 174, 177, 180–89, 191, 193–95, 198–202, 205–7
Cerrig-y-drudion 145
changeling 9, 76, 94–96, 98, 101, 109, 111-2, 116, 123, 141
charms 2, 7, 8, 12, 14, 21, 44, 45, 61, 65, 69, 74, 79, 83, 84, 98, 123, 128, 129, 132, 140, 141, 146, 147, 158, 159, 172, 174, 177, 178, 183–85, 187, 189–92, 198–207
cheese 54, 119, 130, 180, 200

Cheshire 158
chicken 25, 107, 125, 127, 135, 195
chimney 120, 121, 147, 154
Christianity 4, 61, 75, 88, 132
churn 10, 180, 182–85, 187, 189, 196–99, 205
circle 4, 5, 25, 33, 35, 62, 65, 66, 68, 81, 94-6, 100, 108, 109, 111, 112, 114, 118, 125, 126, 128, 135, 139, 145, 192, 198, 201
cloth 25, 27, 81, 117, 118, 121, 125, 135, 220, 221
clwyd 144, 146, 162
coal 1, 8
cockerel 35, 64, 65, 160, 176
commandments 71
Conwy 145
correspondences 148
countermagic 155, 194
cows 102, 108, 114, 185, 188, 194–96, 200, 202, 206
cursing 2, 10, 145-6, 150, 154–57, 162, 163, 165-8, 172, 176, 185-6, 197, 225, 227-9
Cwrt-y-cadno 2, 3, 13, 86, 87, 91, 194

Dafydd ap Gwilym 79, 89-90
dairy 130, 185, 186, 197, 198
Daniel 52
Dauis, Dauydd (Dafydd Dafis) 131-3
dead 12, 21, 46–48, 51, 64, 71, 72, 75, 96, 110, 131, 159, 160, 180, 181, 193, 195, 217, 224
death 52, 71, 73, 145, 149, 161, 163, 174, 176, 178, 190
demon 60, 83, 85, 88, 91, 140, 142, 153, 154, 178, 229
devil 75, 119, 152, 153, 197, 229
Devonshire 73
Dinbych 148, 152, 154, 217, 223
disease 81, 158, 176, 183, 189–92, 196, 202, 205, 229
diviners 177
dogs 195

donkey 195, 196
drink 61, 65, 126, 167, 193, 228
druids 71, 75
dwarfs 97-8, 103-4

earth 28, 46, 48, 68, 71, 72, 89, 103, 127, 134, 135, 137, 140, 191, 193, 194, 208
Ecclesiastes 224
Edwart, Ellis 131–33, 140
eggshell 94, 96, 98, 103
Egypt 4-8, 158
eisteddfod 4, 6
Elidorus, Elidyr 76, 77, 89
elves 79, 97
Emannuel 72, 200
Enchanters 89, 91
enchantments 3
enchantress 132
Evans-Wentz, Walter 86, 89, 91

fairies 1, 7, 9, 10, 12, 14, 21, 28, 60, 63, 64, 71, 75, 76, 79–94, 96–98, 100–102, 106, 109, 111–23, 126, 127, 129–31, 135–37, 140, 146, 185, 186, 198
Ffestiniog 95
Ffynnon Elian 2, 10, 144, 154–56, 165–67, 172, 173, 225, 227, 228
Ffynnon Tegla 165, 228
Flintshire 54, 144, 145, 162, 166, 170, 173, 180
Fraich-y-Ddinas 141
fraud 1, 10, 80, 83, 87, 91, 138, 146, 156, 165, 173

Garthbeibio 174-5
geese 176, 193
geomancy 21, 71, 208–14

ghosts 52, 71, 74, 101, 102, 131, 137, 138, 152-4, 158, 167, 189, 192, 202, 219
Glamorgan 61, 101, 144
Glasynys (Owen Wynne Jones) 119
goat 149, 195
goblin 95–98, 123
gold 33, 62, 77, 80, 82, 112, 118, 211, 221
Gomer 89
greyhounds 77
grimoire 74, 83, 86, 127, 198
guinea-pig 151
Gwarwyn-a-throt 106, 107

Harms, Daniel 60, 88, 91, 126, 129, 140-1
Harries, John (see also Cwrt-y-cadno) 2, 3, 13, 86, 87, 89, 177, 195
Heptameron 74, 126
herbs 21, 44, 45, 69, 128, 178, 184
Hockley, Frederick 60, 71, 128
Holyhead 110
Hugh 84, 85, 110

Ifan 111
incantations 12, 87, 127, 158
invisibility 7, 74, 84, 88, 128, 131, 207
invocation 1, 12, 21, 35, 46, 71, 83, 126, 135–38
Iolo Morganwg 119
Ireland 11, 89, 93, 117, 141
Italy 128

Jacob 52, 73, 128
Jesus Christ 27, 48, 52, 69, 72, 73, 136, 137, 140, 190–92, 200–202, 209

kabbalah 65
knives 120, 126

Langybi 85
lard 65
Lenihan, Eddie 88
Llanfabon 96, 101-2, 116, 123
Llanfihangel 229
Llanfrothen 148, 187
Llangurig 197, 206
Llanrhaedr-ym-Mochnant 149
Llansilin 174, 189, 206
Llanvaglan 82, 90
Llyfr Dewiniaeth 64, 126, 132-3, 199
London 13, 60, 132, 133, 151, 159, 206

Mabinogi 78
Madziarczyk 214
Maentwrog 229
Magdalen 191, 218
maid 106, 107, 114, 115, 121, 158
manuscript 1, 3, 12, 50, 61, 71, 73, 91, 119, 127, 128, 133, 140, 172, 189, 199, 211, 227
marigold 35, 64
Meilyr 88
Meiob/Micob/Micol/Micopau 26, 27, 83, 125, 127-9, 140
mercury 44, 45, 69, 178
Mercurii 69
Merlin 211
Methodism 93, 156
milk 54, 77, 90, 106, 107, 120, 126, 170, 180, 182, 183, 185, 187, 188, 199, 200, 202, 205, 217
mining 33, 63-4, 154
minerals 33, 62

Montgomeryshire 13, 149, 165, 178, 189, 191, 193, 197, 199, 201, 205, 206
moon 21, 28, 31, 42, 52, 54, 61, 68, 73, 77, 102–4, 108, 109, 117, 118, 120, 121, 137-8, 158, 159, 164, 166, 167, 208, 210
Morgan 116, 195
murder 100, 113, 146, 153, 229

Napoleon 211
Nasruddin 186, 206
Nazis 4- 5
necromancy 21, 50, 51, 72, 73, 153, 172
nonconformist 4, 6, 171, 175, 189
nutshell 117

oath 112, 191
oats 97
 140
Oberian/Oberion/Oberon 26, 27, 125, 127, 135, 140
occultism 60, 71, 74, 125, 126, 128, 140, 197, 208-9, 211, 214
ointment 224
Owen, Elias 96, 123, 159, 162, 173-4, 178-9, 184, 186, 189, 206
Owen, Morfudd 13
oxen 108
Oxford 5, 60

pacifism 6
pagan 175
pail 117, 118, 120
Palmistry 12, 82, 90
Paracletus 201
parchment 35, 65, 167, 176

pebble 155, 157
Pembrokeshire 88, 206
Penardd (John Humphrey Davies) 132-3, 231
Philosophical 211
pigs 176, 185, 192, 202
planets 40, 60-1, 66, 147, 176, 177, 198, 208, 210
pony 193
pottage 94, 97
Powys 96, 183
Psalms 65, 166, 228
pwca 107
pygmies 75, 83, 127

Rankine, David 63, 88, 133
Raphael 69, 71, 172, 214
rhamanta 74
rheibio 176
Rhiannon 78
rhinwedd 190
Rhosesmor 165, 166, 168, 170–73, 178, 225, 228
Rhys Ddwfn 90, 110
Rhŷs, Sir John 14, 94-5, 98, 109, 111, 123, 141
Roberts, Robert 140-2
Ruabon 157, 163, 226, 227

Sabaoth 65, 200-1
Sarabotas 56, 57, 62, 74
Satan 153, 229
Sathan 34, 35
Sator Arepo 21, 28, 29, 61, 137, 140
Scandinavia 128, 129, 141
Seryddiaeth 74, 126, 140, 142, 210
Shakespeare 127, 176
shoemaker 168, 171
shoes 147

Shon Rhosemor 10, 54, 74, 156, 164-168, 174–76, 178, 186
Shrewsbury 176
Shropshire 158
Sian 148, 218
Siôn Gyfarwydd 164–66, 168, 170–78, 225, 229
Sioned Gorn 144, 147–49, 152, 218, 228
sisters 1, 8, 9, 27, 29, 60–62, 65, 79, 125, 127–29, 131–41, 195, 199, 207
Solomon 52, 73, 198, 207
Somerset 117
spells 1, 7, 12, 60, 69, 71, 92, 130, 147, 148, 161, 184, 200, 205, 211
spinning 106, 107
squirrel 151, 220
Starling, Mhara 12
Suggett, Richard 12, 89, 91, 154, 162, 169, 178, 207
Swansea 3–6, 12, 13, 91

tailor 147, 171
Taliesin 91, 119
Testunau Swyngyfaredd 62, 64, 126, 132-3, 139
Tetragrammaton 65, 72, 73
thief 52, 69, 73, 111, 140, 147, 153, 158–60, 174-5, 185, 186, 220, 222, 226
Tongue, Ruth 123
treasure 27, 35, 62–64, 76, 79, 87, 91, 127-8, 129, 131, 133-8
Tregaron 113
Tylwyth Teg 1, 7, 9, 12, 21, 24–27, 30–35, 63, 64, 71, 75, 76, 78–81, 83- 87, 89–93, 97, 99, 109, 111, 127, 130, 141

unwitching 10, 55, 74, 148, 168, 176-7, 180, 184-6

Wellcome 5, 6, 61
Welshpool 202
Worcester 169

www.ingramcontent.com/pod-product-compliance
Lightning Source LLC
Chambersburg PA
CBHW030256100526
44590CB00012B/421